THE
MINDS
OF
MEN

AN AMERICAN INTELLIGENCE BRIEF

ERIC SANDERS
AUTHOR

Gotham Books
30 N Gould St.
Ste. 20820, Sheridan, WY 82801
https://gothambooksinc.com/
Phone: 1 (307) 464-7800

© 2022 Eric Sanders. All rights reserved.
No part of this book may be reproduced, stored in a retrieval system,
or transmitted by any means without the
written permission of the author.

Published by Gotham Books (August 16, 2022)

ISBN: 979-8-88775-021-7 P
ISBN: 979-8-88775-022-4 E

Any people depicted in stock imagery provided by iStock
are models, and such images are being used for illustrative purposes only.

Certain stock imagery © iStock.

Because of the dynamic nature of the Internet, any web addresses,
or links contained in this book may have changed since publication and
may no longer be valid. The views expressed in this work are solely those
of the author and do not necessarily reflect the views of the publisher,
and the publisher hereby disclaims any responsibility for them.

Table of CONTENTS

01	I.	For What Purpose
27	II.	A Grim Revelation
41	III.	Money At The Root
46	IV.	The Great and Terrible Depression
52	V.	The Calm Before The Storm
65	VI.	The Kennedy Era
75	VII.	The Secret Services
86	VIII.	A War on Guns
95	IX.	Consider the Constitution
101	X.	The Banks and Their Agents
106	XI.	The Great Recession of 2007
115	XII.	The Grassy Knoll
120	XIII.	The New Money
131	XIV.	The Creditors

I
For What Purpose

There are universal questions that tempt our minds unto jealousy, and cause doubt to rear its divisive head. However, these questions are also the reason why men and women look up to divinity and ask, plead and cry out for truth, for revelation. They are these: "What are the right questions to ask upon considering the existence of man? Where do we go to find the answers? Also, how will we know that we have the answers to life's questions once they are before us? In the beginning the earth was void and without form, yet the Spirit of God was there and moved upon the waters. The first commandment of God proclaimed upon the earth was "Let there be light!" (Genesis 1: 1-3) Then God created in the heavens on behalf of the earth three main sources of light that would chase out the darkness. They are namely the sun, moon, and stars. (Genesis 1: 14-18) Until such lights were brought unto the earth life was not breathed into any creature or any other soon-to-be living thing upon thing upon the earth. God is the founder of all light and life in the universe. To be like God we must learn to divide the light from the dark in order to see the truth of all things. We must learn to drink deeply of the well springs from which the living waters flow, living water which leads to the tree of life along the narrow path of salvation. It is our purpose to discover, to learn, to remember who we are, from whence and from whom we are. It is our duty to find our way unto that path that will lead us unto a glorious return and reunion unto that God who gave us life.

One of the keys to understanding who we are not only in the study of our creator, but is further uncovered in gaining a healthy, distant respect unto whence, whom and how we are not. There is a defining, character altering power that allows a man or woman to change, to become like the God we choose to serve and follow after; that power is love. The scriptures declare, "For as Charity is the pure love of Christ", then its antithesis, "Mahan", is the self- destructive love of Lucifer. (Moroni 7: 16) Let us begin with a study of the life of Cain and how he fell from grace, and subsequently became "Master Mahan", even a "Son of Perdition". Adam knew his wife Eve and bare a son, their first-born and named him Cain. Cain was a tiller of the ground by profession. Abel, Cain's little brother, was a keeper of sheep. "In the process of time it came to pass, that Cain brought of the ground an offering unto the Lord. And Abel he also brought of the firstlings of his flock and of the fat thereof. And the Lord had respect unto Able." (Genesis 4: 3-4) For some significant reason the Lord had not respect unto Cain's offering, but why not? First consider that the Lord looks on the heart and trieth the reins. It is evident that something in Cain's character, Cain's heart was amiss. Therefore, Cain was not ready for the blessing Abel merited at that time, which was the Priesthood of God. That is an incredible understatement as we will discover yet. Though, we can always count on the Lord to counsel with us and even offers comfort, despite our rebellious tendencies. The Lord encouraged Cain on this wise: "But unto Cain and to his offering he had not respect. And Cain was very wroth, and his countenance fell. And the Lord said unto Cain, why art thou wroth? And why is thy countenance fallen? If thou do well, shalt thou are not accepted?"

(Genesis 4: 5-7) Then, a word of omniscient counsel was imparted to Cain by the Lord: "And if thou doest not well, sin liest at the door. And unto thee shall be his desire, and thou shalt rule over him." (Genesis 4: 7) There is an insight into why Cain was so tremendously distressed by the outcome of these events, leading up to the initial rejection of his offering. We read in Moses 5: 18-21, "And Cain loved Satan more than God. And Satan commanded him, saying: Make an offering unto the Lord. But unto Cain, and unto his offering, he had not respect. Now Satan knew this, and it pleased him." What was Cain's response to the Lord's counsel? In verse 25 it is revealed unto whom Cain's heart felt sway, wherefore Cain loved Satan more than God. Not just Cain, but also those who loved Cain began to fall as well.

After Adam and Eve taught the plan of salvation unto their children Satan came among them. (Moses 5:12) In verse 13 we continue: "And Satan came among them, saying: I also am a Son of God; and he commanded them, saying: believe it (the plan of salvation) not; and they believed it not, and they loved Satan more than God. And men began from that time forth to be carnal, sensual, and devilish." These are three attributes, or characteristics of he or she who loves Satan more than God, who follow after Mahan and whose belly desires mammon. Carnality, Sensuality and Devilishness are manifested further in Cain's official fall from grace which was sealed on earth as it is in heaven as we read in Moses 5, verses 28-34: "And it came to pass that Cain took one of his brother's daughters to wife, and they loved Satan more than God. And Satan said unto Cain: Swear unto me by thy throat, and if thou tell it thou shalt die; and swear thy brethren by their heads, and thy living God, that they tell it not; for if they tell it, they shall surely die; and this that thy father may not know it; and this day I will deliver thy brother Abel into thy hands." Adam, (Cain and Abel's father) is also known as the same Michael, the Arc Angel who led the battle against Satan, or Lucifer during our pre-earth existence in response to the Adversary declaring war in heaven, leading away a third of the hosts thereof. (Revelations 12: 7) It is very apparent and a certain reality that Satan and those same host of heaven are warring still against the sons of Adam and daughters of Eve. The fight with sin is as real today as it ever was. In verse 30 of Moses 5 we continue: "And Satan sware unto Cain that he would do according to his commands. And all these things were done in secret. And Cain said: Truly I am Mahan, the master of this great secret, that I may murder and get gain. Wherefore, Cain was called Master Mahan, and he gloried in his wickedness. And Cain went into the field and Cain talked with Abel, his brother. And it came to pass while they were in the field, Cain rose up against Abel, his brother, and slew him. And Cain gloried in that which he had done, saying: I am free. And the Lord said unto Cain: Where is Abel, thy brother? And he said: I know not, am I my brother's keeper?" The Lord shifts gears and gets to the heart of the matter and Cain confesses. Then, the Lord lowers the eternal boom, a curse that would be everlasting fell upon Cain at his word. Cain's reply was

"My punishment is more than I can bear." Such will be the replies of all of the sons of perdition. They will have to confess all of their sins to the Lord, and they too will feel their punishment . . . however terrible, however endless . . . will be more than they can bear. We obtain a mighty glimpse at how Lucifer fell, before the world was and why the war still rages, upon considering the following: "Wherefore because that Satan rebelled against me, and sought to destroy the agency of man, which I, the Lord God had given him, also, that I should give unto him my own power; by the power of mine only begotten, I caused that he should be cast down.

And he became Satan, yea, even the devil, the father of all lies to deceive and to blind men, and to lead them captive at his will, even as many as would not hearken unto my voice." (Moses 4: 3-4) Jehovah, our Redeemer, our Savior, the Christ stood against Lucifer before the Father, Elohim and chose to submit his will to the father's. Lucifer's plan collaborated certain aspects of the plan of salvation, such as Jesus's suffering for mankind's sins, pains, and injustices; but the glory would not be unto the Father, rather unto himself. His bargaining tool, so he thought, was utilizing the agency of one third of all heavenly hosts against themselves, betting that the Father would not cast out so many of his children collectively. It is true that the Father did grieve over losing so many of his children of light to darkness and error. However, his plan is the only way back home unto exaltation for all of his likeness; yea, the spirits of just men made perfect. Jehovah demonstrated before the foundations of the earth that he was willing to do the Father's will even if it meant giving his life. Lucifer, in contrast, demanded the Father do his will even if it meant giving Jehovah's life. Jehovah's attitude was submissive, Lucifer's attitude was manipulative. Jehovah, because of his sacrifice and obedience was able to obtain all that the Father hath and provided the way for man on earth to achieve the same latitude by following after the Savior's example. Lucifer, due to his disobedience and pride was cast out of the Father's presence and tragically took an expansive host of his brothers and sisters down with him. This is a stark, horrifying reality which results from having sympathy for the devil. How does the adversary bind the souls of men on earth? Let us read in Moses 5: 47-51 which describes how these destructive traditions of men were passed down in families, the children of Cain: And Lamech (grandson of Cain) said unto his wives, Adah, and Zillah: Hear my voice, ye wives of Lamech, hearken unto my speech; for I have slain a man to my wounding, and a young man to my hurt. If Cain be avenged sevenfold, truly Lamech shall be seventy and seven-fold; For Lamech having entered into a covenant with Satan, after the manner of Cain, wherein became Master Mahan, master of that great secret which was administered unto Cain by Satan; and Irad, (son of Cain), having known their secret, began to reveal it unto the sons of Adam. Wherefore, Lamech, being angry slew him, not like unto Cain his brother Abel, for the sake of getting gain, but he slew him for the oath's sake. For, from the days of Cain, there was a secret combination, and their works were in the dark, and they knew every man, his brother." This is the same secret combination which through its administration Satan was able infiltrate and collapse from the inside out the Nephite nation of ancient America. We read of such in the Book of Mormon, which coincidentally is written specifically as a mode, a pattern for our day and time, chalk full of collective and individual do's and don'ts. One of three traits or fruits that demonstrate charity is not in someone or in a group is that Cain, for example, gloried in his wickedness, his wicked collusion and design preceding the assassination of one of the Lord's anointed, his own brother, Abel. However, in 1 Corinthians 13: 6 it states regarding Charity, that it "rejoiceth not in iniquity, but rejoiceth in the truth." Two impactful results occur due to the actions of those who compact, or oath with Lucifer, thus dedicating themselves to the destruction of a nation. First, the men or women who are so aligned work in the dark, at first. They infiltrate governments, businesses, educational institutions, religious institutions, and the media until they begin to dominate and control them one by one. It is through these institutions that secret combinations attack the morality of the masses. They introduce immorality and lasciviousness as popular, socially acceptable, and finally moral and beraid anyone who would shed light on the darkness behind their passionate mission (to be free at the expense of enslaving all mankind) by vilification and misrepresentation. In the Book of Helaman 2: 4-5 it relates the story of how secret combinations were intermingled into ancient American societies, it reads: "For there was one Gadianton, who was exceedingly expert in many words, and also in his craft, to carry on the secret work of murder and of robbery . . . . therefore, he became the leader of the band of Kishkumen. Therefore, he did flatter them, and also Kishkumen, that if they would place him in the judgment seat, he would grant unto those who belonged to his band that they should be placed in power and authority among the people; therefore, Kishkumen sought to destroy Helaman." Helaman, an ancient American prophet, was next in line to become the chief judge among the Nephite nation. Thankfully for Helaman, Gadianton's perilous plot was discovered and Kishkumen was killed. However, Gadianton and his band of robbers escaped judgment and fled. Where did they go? In Helaman 3: 23 (about 5 years later) states the following: "And it came to pass in the forty and ninth year of the reign of the judges, there was continual peace established in the land, all save it were the secret combinations which Gadianton the robber had established in the more settled parts of the land, which at that time were not known unto those who were at the head of government; therefore they were not destroyed out of the land." As we read further along in Helaman 6: 16-18 we find how Gadianton infused his influence into both the Nephite and Lamanite nations and turned them against one another, it reads: "And in the commencement of the sixty and seventh year (about 27 B.C.) the people began to grow exceedingly wicked again. For behold, the Lord had blessed them so long with the riches of the world that they had not been stirred up to anger, to wars, nor to bloodshed; therefore, they began to set their hearts upon their riches; yea, they began to commit secret murders, and to rob and plunder, that they might get gain. And now behold, those murderers and plunderers were a band who had been formed by Kishkumen and Gadianton. And now it came to pass that there were many, even among the Nephites, of Gadianton's band. But behold, they were more numerous among the more wicked part of the Lamanites. And they were called the Gadianton Robbers and Murderers." In the process of time the Gadianton Robbers of both nations began to unite. They established their secret oaths and signs and key words to distinguish a brother from someone else and this practice was commonplace in the event a brother had been caught in a crime, whereas, in accord with the oath did escape judgment. In verses 26-27 of the same chapter, we find: "Now behold, those secret oaths and covenants did not come forth unto Gadianton from the records which were delivered unto Helaman; but behold, they were put into the heart of Gadianton by that same being who did entice our first parents to partake of the forbidden fruit. Yea, that same being who did plot with Cain, that if he would murder his brother Abel it should not be known unto the world. And he did plot with Cain and his followers from that time forth." Since the Gadianton Robbers had not been made extinct they continued to pass down their secret oaths and covenants unto their posterity within the Nephite and Lamanite nations. Fast-forward to roughly 550-600 A.D. on the ancient American continent and we will take a glimpse at what effect this band eventually had upon the people. Mormon, an ancient American prophet for whom the book of Mormon is named, recorded: "And I did endeavor to preach unto this people, but my mouth was shut, and I was forbidden that I should preach unto them; for behold they had willfully rebelled against their God.

But I did remain among them, but I was forbidden to preach unto them because of the hardness of their hearts. And these Gadianton Robbers who were among the Lamanites, did infest the land, insomuch that the inhabitants thereof began to hide their treasures in the earth; and they became slippery, because the Lord had cursed the land, that they could not hold them nor retain them again. And it came to pass that there were sorceries and witchcrafts and majics; and the power of the evil one was wrought upon all the face of the land, even unto the fulfilling of all the words of Abinadi, and also Samuel, the Lamanite." (Mormon 1: 16-19) Now, going back to the Eastern Hemisphere, Israel, between 1 A.D. and 33 A.D., let's carefully consider this question: "Did Satan conspire in the hearts of men like unto the oath made with Cain, Lamech or even Gadianton in Jerusalem during the life, ministry and establishment of Christ's Church and Order anciently?" Let us begin in John 8 and read the words of the Savior concerning the matter; in verses 34-45 (Jesus preaching unto a crowd of Jews) respectively, he states: "Verily, verily, I say unto you whosoever committeth sin is the servant of sin. And the servant abideth not in the house forever: but the Son abideth ever. If the Son therefore shall make you free, ye shall be free indeed. I know that ye are Abraham's seed: but ye seek to kill me, because my word hath no place in you. I speak that which I have seen with my Father: and ye do that which ye have seen with your father. They answered and said unto him, Abraham is our father. Jesus saith unto them, if ye were Abraham's children, ye would do the works of Abraham. Ye do the deeds of your father. Then they said unto him, we be not born of fornication; we have one father, even God. Jesus said unto them, if God were your father, ye would love me: for I proceeded forth and came from God; neither came I of myself, but he sent me.

Why do ye not understand my speech? even because ye cannot hear my word. Ye are of your father the devil, and the lusts of your father ye will do. He was a murderer from the beginning, and abode not in the truth, because there is no truth in him. When he speaketh a lie, he speaketh of his own: for he is a liar and the father of it. And because I tell you the truth ye believe me not." At about 30 A.D., shortly following the baptism of Jesus by his cousin, John the Baptist, the Savior's ministry begins. Yet, John's is coming to a violent close. In Mathew 4, verses 12, 14, and 16-17 we read: "Now when Jesus had heard that John was cast into prison, he departed into Galilee. That It might be fulfilled which was spoken by Esaias (Isaiah) the prophet, saying: The people who sat in darkness saw a great light; and to them which sat in the region and shadow of death light is sprung up." In Mathew 23, verses 33 and 35 contain the words of the Lord regarding murderous conspirator's treatment of prophets, his anointed since the beginning: "ye serpents, ye generation of vipers, how can ye escape the damnation of hell. That upon you may come all the righteous blood shed upon the earth, from the blood of righteous Abel unto the blood of Zacharias (father of John the Baptist, Jesus' uncle), son of Barchais, whom ye slew between the temple and the altar." Zacharias was slain under the order of King Herod as a result of his courage to stay silent regarding the whereabouts of his firstborn son, John the Baptist. Such was the aftermath following Herod's order for all first-born children to be slain in the land, male and female. The book of Mark, chapter 6 tells of the belated martyrdom of John the Baptist which unfolds in verses 18 and 20-28; wherein John the Baptist boldly declares Herod's recent marriage an abomination before God: "It is not lawful for thee to have thy brother's wife . . . For Herod feared John, knowing that he was a just man. And when a convenient day was come, that Herod on his birthday made a supper to his Lords, high captains, and chief estates of Galilee; and when the daughter of the said Herodias came in, and danced, and pleased Herod and them that sat with him, the king said unto the damsel, ask of me whatsoever thou wilt, and I will give it thee. And he sware unto her. And she went forth and said unto her mother, what shall I ask? And she said, the head of John the Baptist. And she came in straightway with haste unto the King, and asked, saying, I will that thou give me by and by in a charger the head of John the Baptist. And the King was exceedingly sorry; yet for his oath's sake, and for their sakes which sat with him, he would not reject her. And immediately the King sent the executioner. And brought his head in a charger and gave it to the damsel; and the damsel gave it to her mother." This oath of murder made by Herod, a government official at the highest level, in the company of affiliated and related individuals is a sign that the practice of secret combinations were in significant prominence and power during Jesus' ministry. It explains how the order of Melchizedec, and Preisthood of Aaron fell, and along with it the authority to act, bind and seal on earth as it is in heaven, in the name of God and such be recorded on earth as it is in heaven for eternity. Jesus, the Christ was sold to the Pharisees for 40 pieces of silver, representative of the ultimate betrayal by one of his own anointed, Judas Iscariot's oath to turn the Savior over to his false accusers with a kiss. This act of Judas also set the stage for the martyrdom of the Apostles and many other true followers of Jesus Christ. The inception and introduction of the dark ages, occurring at roughly 100 A.D., was simultaneous to the fall of the primitive church; hence, the Great Apostasy. Therefore, the absolute necessity for a latter-day restoration of the authority and order of Christ's original church and organization was deemed paramount. Judas Iscariot fell to the hangman's noose as he cast judgment upon himself for his crime against the Master, Jesus of Nazareth.

It is clearly evident that his unbearable shame stemmed from what he understood, his eternal punishment was more than he could live with, more than he could bear. The Savior, following his three days prophecy, returned unto his beloved ones, Mary Magdalene and then the Apostles. To his downtrodden, distraught disciples he declared "Ought not Christ to have suffered these things, and enter into his glory? Peace be unto you. Why are ye troubled? And why do thoughts arise in your hearts? Behold my hands and my feet, that it is I, myself: handle me, and see; for a spirit hath not flesh and bones, as ye see me have. These are the words which I spake unto you, that all things must be fulfilled, which were written in the law of Moses, and in the psalms, concerning me. And ye are witnesses of these things." (Luke 24: 26, 36, 38-39) The Christ is not the first martyr upon the earth, Abel being the first; and certainly not the last. Jesus is Chief among them, however and bowed himself below all things; even the martyrs throughout all time, he being the Chief Cornerstone. The martyrs paid their most lowly and fully meted devotion to their Chief Exemplar and Ever- living Head and counted themselves unworthy servants still. Their offering was a devotion paid to the Most High no man can put a price on! So, a question we may ask in repose and reverence to the innocent who die in the name of the Lord is "why were they killed?" Depending upon your point of view you may see different reasons why. However, from the perspective of "Mahan" there is a central theme the reasons always point to: "Freedom". After Cain became "Master Mahan", following the martyrdom of his brother, Abel, he, Cain, was moved to exclaim: "I am Free!" The participants in secret combinations: the perpetrators, administrators, and conspirators are all bought and sold on the version of free agency Satan is selling. Such leaves them un beholden to the rules of society, the laws of man and most unflinchingly the laws of God.

Whereas they follow the dictates of their own conscious, or complete lack thereof; their love having waxed cold, save it be love for Perdition (Mahan) and unto those who endeavor to be his sons. For example, in 1419 A.D., one Sir John Oldcastle, Lord Cobham, was accused of heresy for his commitment to the teachings of John Wickliffe. In his own defense prior to his martyrdom Lord Cobham declared: ""As for images, I understand that they be not of belief, but that they were ordained since the belief of Christ was given by sufferance of the Church, to represent and bring to mind the passion of our Lord Jesus Christ, and martyrdom and good living of other saints: and that whoso it be, that doth the worship to dead images that is due to God, or putteth such hope or trust in help of them, as he should do to God, or hath affection in one more than in another, he doth in that, the greatest sin of idol worship . . . . Also, I suppose this fully, that every man in this earth is a pilgrim toward bliss, or toward pain; and that he that knoweth not, we will not know, we keep the holy commandments of God in his living here (albeit that he go on pilgrimages to all the world, and he die so), he shall be damned: he that knoweth the holy commandments of God, and keepeth them to his end, he shall be saved, though he never in his life go on pilgrimage, as men now use, to Canterbury, or to Rome, or to any other place." Lord Cobham praised God until no further life was left in him, as he hung in chains and was burned alive unto his death. To offer pertinent background we should gander a few more excerpts from Foxe's Book of the Martyrs. For instance, John Wickliff (whom Lord Cobham was deeply influenced by) served Pope Gregory XI (1377) as Rector of Lutterworth in the Diocese of Lincoln and was also a professor of divinity at University of Oxford in England. (pp 58) Collected from the Articles of John Wickliff's sermons a bold view of life under the auspices of Papal rule comes to light.

Whereas Wickliff declares his stance against the Papacy's medieval dictatorship during his day: "1. The Gospel is a rule sufficient of itself to rule the life of every Christian man here, without any other rule. 2. All other rules, under whose observances divers religious persons be governed, do add no more perfection to the Gospel, then doth the white colour to the wall. 3. Neither the Pope, nor any other prelate of the church, ought to have prisons wherein to punish transgressors." (pp 57) This teaching soon was discovered and brought before Pope Gregory XI in Rome, as well as King Richard II in London, England. Such was considered "detestable folly" by the monarchies aforementioned and as a result Wickliff was forced into hiding but died in peace 1384 A.D. Wickliff was "buried in his own parish church at Lutterworth in Leicestershire." (pp57) Upon reviewing all of the grave enemies and persecutors of Wickliff for his doctrine, the clergy of the Papacy grieved him the most. Yet his works and teachings lived on in the adamant hearts and minds of fearless nobles such as Sir John Oldcastle, Knight, Lord Cobham, leader of the Lollards. On one occasion King Richard II called upon Lord Cobham to meet with him privily and did earnestly admonish Sir John to submit himself to the rule of the "Mother Church." However, it was not in Lord Cobham's bones to turn against those evidentiary truths he had then embraced in exchange for a favor of expediency from the Pope of Rome (who Sir John held as the "Antichrist of Europe"). (pp 70) As a result, the Archbishop laid articles against Lord Cobham, Sir John Oldcastle, Knight, and Leader of the Lollards. In response, Lord Cobham sought relief from King Richard II in prose. Nonetheless, the king refused his plea for mercy, to his woeful surprise. Sir John, a noble and peer to the King was left no recourse but to either deny his new-found faith or perish. On the 23rd of September 1413 'A.D. Sir John arrived in the custody of Sir Robert Morely, Knight, at his appointed "examination" before Thomas Arundel, Archbishop and two other Bishops (Richard Clifford of London and Henry Boliabrook of Winchester). Sir John, it is important to note, was for his beliefs found guilty by the Mother Church of certain heresies prior to this occasion, but was escaped of judgment until this time. Sir John was given opportunity to explain to his accusers regarding his position against idol worship, thus, referring the Bishops to the 10 Commandments received by Moses, written by the hand of God. Lord Cobham's testimony continues, in summary, as follows: "that he would gladly both believe and observe whatever holy church of Christ's institution had determined, or yet whatever God had willed him either to believe or to do but that the Pope of Rome, with his cardinals, archbishops, bishops, and other prelates of that church, had lawful power to determine such matter as stood not with his word thoroughly, that, would he not at that time affirm." (pp 70) Therefore, Lord Cobham was granted until the 25th of September 1413 A.D. to affirm his allegiances, either for or against the Mother Church. On the appointed day in question, before a host of "priests, monks, friars, parish clerks, bell-ringers, and pardoners, Sir Robert Morley, Knight and Lieutenant of the Tower," brought Sir John Oldcastle, Lord Cobham before his accusers once more, as "a lamb among wolves." (pp 70) Lord Cobham answered their stern accusations as boldly as any man could, he proclaimed: "My belief is, that all the scriptures of the sacred Bible are true . . . but in your lordly laws and idle determinations have I no belief. For ye be no part of Christ's Holy Church, as your deeds do openly show; but ye are very Antichrists, obstinately set against His Holy law and will." (pp 78) Following a barrage of poignant, searching questions by his accusers and then courageous declarations by Lord Cobham in reply he finally declared in sincere demonstration of his conviction, "do with me what you will." (pp 82).

Thereafter, Sir John was taken to the tower by Sir Robert Morley for a short period of time. Though, Lord Cobham made a way for escape and traveled throughout Europe bearing his testimony and utilizing his new-found zeal to minister on his way to Wales. There he found refuge with one Lord Powis, with whom Lord Cobham remained until 1417. Unfortunately, Lord Powis, once a noble friend to Lord Cobham, later turned Judas and gave him back into the hands of judgment (the Royal Crown of England, in league with the Papacy). Sir John Oldcastle, Lord Cobham, Knight, and leader of the Lollards was executed in St. Giles Field of London, England. It is said that Lord Cobham arrived cheerfully. (pp 88) Converts to the Church of Jesus Christ of Latter-Day Saints in the 1830's and 1840's felt the oppressive power of organized men in government, in commerce, touching every aspect of their personal lives. There were conspirators, evil judges, corrupt lawmen (or lawless men), angry mobs, angry ministers, and persecutors of righteous men of God at the heads of government during Joseph Smith, Jr.'s (Prophet and President of the church, 1830-1844) day and time. For reasons of politics, of jealousy, of unwarranted fears, and because of the influence of the adversary in the hearts and minds of men, whose souls were riddled with greed and hate, the people of God were robbed of their God-given liberties under the Constititution for the United States. The saints were brutalized, raped, murdered, driven from their homes, their businesses, and the government (local, state, and federal) never brought a single one of the guilty to justice. Not to mention, the media held up the actions of these fiends as honorable and brave. They were, however, Bullies! Thieves! Cowards! Murderers! They served perdition and will yet pay for their crimes against humanity, the innocent. For every knee shall bow and every tongue confess God's judgments are just. The extreme deficit in the local, state, and federal protections to members of the church eventually led to the incarceration and murder of the prophet Joseph Smith, Jr. and his brother Hyrum in Carthage Jail, Illinois. We read regarding the official response and record of the church to these crimes in Doctrine and Covenants, section 134, verses 3-4: "Joseph Smith, the prophet and seer of the Lord, has done more, save Jesus only, for the salvation of men in the world, than any other man that ever lived in it. He left a fame and a name that cannot be slain. He lived great, he died great in the eyes of God and his people; and like most of the Lord's anointed in ancient times, has sealed his mission and his works with his own blood; and so, has his brother Hyrum. In life they were not divided, and in death they were not separated. When Joseph went to Carthage to deliver himself up to the pretended requirements of the law, two or three days previous to his assassination, he said: "I am going like a lamb to the slaughter; but I am as calm as a summer's morning; I have a conscious void of offense towards God, and towards all men. I shall die____ innocent, and it shall yet be said of me—he was murdered in cold blood." In verse 6 we continue: "If the fire can scathe a green tree for the glory of God, how easy it will burn up the dry trees to purify the vineyard of corruption. They lived for glory; they died for glory; and glory is their eternal reward." In Doctrine in Covenants section 18, verses 10-13 we learn why the Lord draws men unto him: "Remember the worth of souls is great in the sight of God; for behold, the Lord your Redeemer suffered death in the flesh; wherefore he suffered the pain of all men that all men might repent and come unto him. And he hath risen again from the dead that he might bring all men unto him, on conditions of repentance. And how great is his joy in the soul that repenteth!" So, who does the Lord fight for, and at the same time, who does he, and those who follow him fight against? Every soul who repents has the Lord's protection. Those who willfully, knowingly rebel against the light of truth are tendered no such righteous indemnity.

This principle is explained further in Doctrine and Covenants section 18, verse 20: "Contend against no church, save it be the church of the devil." How do we stand against evil and identify such an organization as well as its affiliates? Let us consider 2 Timothy, chapter 2, verses 24-26: "the servant of the Lord must not strive: but be gentle unto all men, apt to teach, patient. In meekness instructing those that oppose themselves, if God peradventure will give them repentance to the acknowledging of the truth; and that they may recover themselves out of the snare of the devil, who are taken captive by him at his will." The church of the devil are collectively those individuals or organizations who would enslave mankind in any form of oppression (unjust rules of law, statutes, and ordinance) or through addictions (drugs, food, gambling, and media) in order to manipulate the path and quality of life for those whom they would thereby ensnare for their own profit and gain, and/or to further their evil designs. Ownership of land, of property coupled with the authority to dictate to subordinate governments and other corporations how to operate and with whom their allegiances must rest primarily, lie with two monarchies in particular—whose firms are bilateral in their representation (Ecclesiastical and Monarchical): they are the Papacy of the Vatican in Rome and the English Royal Crown in London. War on lesser nations is their common royal path to global dominance. Whereas, they have combined their efforts, as well as served to be at odds depending on whose interests were being threatened, in order to achieve independence from one another and power over the masses. I find it of no coincidence, however ironic, that many of the same social ills plaguing England during the 18th and 19th Centuries now run amuck in the U.S. today. During that time period of public moral decay among the Brits, the birth of the reformation began to take shape. For example, evangelicals such as John Wesley helped to bolster spiritual growth sufficient to rise above the injustices taking precedence there, at the inception of the Enlightenment Era. The teaching outside the doctrines of the Mother Church aided to cause the people to look honestly upon their plight that they might "look to God and live" in order to overcome the inherent abuses of the day. A plethora of England's history records with respect to the collective ills of the time as follows: "Corruption and mismanagement in high places were the rule . . . Bribery among all classes was open, unblushing, and profuse . . . adultery, fornication, gambling, swearing, Sabbath breaking, and drunkenness were hardly regarded as vices at all. They were the fashionable practices of the people in the highest ranks of society . . . such was England in the 18th Century." (Stormer, John A., The Death of A Nation, pp 123) There are far worse crimes to consider here, which have been drummed up by the greatest group of collective con artists throughout history, cloaked behind the auspices of representative government, operating on behalf of the sovereign. The dirtiest word in the English language, according to my Psychology 101 professor (a decorated veteran of the Vietnam War) at Daytona State College, is WAR! There are reasons why countries go to war. Not all are made public in the interest of so-called national security. However, it is always in the interest of the government, the sovereign it protects and not on behalf of the people whom it supposedly serves; whereas the people of the nation are (unknowingly) often by contract considered debtors of the State. In fact, the incorporated representative governments of the world would have us indebted, indentured, and enslaved unto them. This has been "accomplished" through the commercialization of the planet under the guise of expressions such as legal, contractual, binding, rules of law and so forth. However, the highest law of the land, being the Constitution and the Bible's written text upon which, in the U.S., it is "For the People" originally intended, are the measuring rod upon which all lesser laws, (local, state, or federal) are held up to or broken against. However, the world is a stage, and everyone has an act to play. Wherefore, with over 10 million different laws currently in force upon this great home of the brave, the question over freedom in this country is beginning to become synonymous with the discourse over who is free and who isn't and why? Many of the wars and rumours of wars have been and will be fought at the feet of infidelity, in the name of freedom! The whole truth is ugly when one considers all of the reasons for going to war. This statement is relevant when we have observed throughout history that the battle for sovereignty has been fought largely at the expense of the lives of the poor, on behalf of those who make laws for our protection. Why do we go to war? Many of the justifications for war were sold to the masses in order to get them on board long enough to win their spirits and contractually gain ownership of them through military service. We shall discuss how the reasons for going to war have been keenly hidden from view. In fact, The Revolutionary War, The War of 1812, The Civil War, WWI, WWII, The Korean Conflict, The Vietnam War, and The Wars in Iraq and Afghanistan cost the best blood our country has to offer for reasons quite the contrary to what was, by our government through public media, sold to the populous as to why they served and why we should go and serve still. Wherefore, many of the wars and rumours of wars have been promulgated through sabotagery, misrepresentation and fraud at the expense of millions of souls who fought the good fight in the name of sovereignty and country. How could we expect anything less than the privations doled to our forefathers by the very Royals whose (this history often is erroneously presented in public schools) Navy and Army defeated our best efforts and last true devotion during the American Revolutionary War. What were those Royal demands upon American Sovereignty which were too burdensome to bear, resulting in such a revolution? British laws being enacted on American soil in order to manipulate the rights and privileges of freedom loving peoples into enslavement. Laws such as The Molasses Act of 1733, The Sugar Act, The Currency Act of 1751, The Stamp Act of 1765, The Quartering Act of 1765, The Townshend Act of 1767, The Restraining Act of 1767, and The Revenue Act of 1767. Unlawful Acts such as these, wholly derivative of foreign influence, were met with boycotts used as a political weapon against our then arch enemy on the other side of the pond. The fight for American independence began April 19, 1775, at the Battle of Concord, MA. "John Adams exhorted the Congress to rise to the "defense of American Liberty" (a Continental Army) and nominated George Washington of Virginia to lead it. Despite the blood that had been shed, a majority in Congress still hoped for reconciliation with Brittan. Yet, Samuel Adams of Massachusetts and Patrick Henry of Virginia mobilized anti-imperial sentiment and won passage of the Declaration of the Causes and Necessities of Taking up Arms. Americans dreaded the "Calamities of Civil War", the declaration asserted, but were "resolved to die free men rather than to live as slaves." In the book "Common Sense" the author Thomas Paine declares a fearless resolve to expose the English Monarchy to the American people in prose. He stated, "Monarchy and Hereditary succession have laid the world in blood and ashes." Paine purported that the monarchy designed three systems of government for three separate classes of people under British rule: There was a government of Kings, a government of Lords, and a government of Commoners. Paine went on to explain, "that it was noble for the dark and slavish times in which it was created", but that now under (crazy) King George III, England was only a "Monarchical tyranny in the person of the King" . . . and . . . "aristocratical tyranny in the person of the peers." (Henretta, James, America's History: Volume 1, fifth ed., pp 166, 167, 168) Though, the Declaration of Independence of 1776 spelled out how Americans desired to emancipate and expatriate from English rule, the Treaty of Paris, 1783, was a result of our agreeing to terms set by Parliament and the Monarchy, rather than fulfillment of separation and perfection of sovereignty. Whereas, the Treaty of Versailles was our acquiescence to British rule and ownership, not their acknowledgement of defeat whatsoever. However, even a bully recognizes the efforts of its victim who stands with a fist ready to fight at any moment's notice and offers such at least a pale amount of thin respect for doing so. As long as commerce resumed its lucrative posture and American politics did not further impede their gluttonous dependence upon our resources in trade, we were permitted to move forward without being completely vanquished from the outside in. In the early 1800's, approximately 1810, it was discovered by the public that the vast majority of banks in the U.S. were owned and controlled by European banking interests, such as the banking behemoth "the House of Rothchild." The American populous was outraged and voiced their concerns to their democratically elected U.S. Congressmen. As a result, on February 10, 1811, Congress allows the **CHARTER FOR THE FIRST BANK OF THE U.S.** to expire. Whereas it was found to be Unconstitutional by Democratic Republicans who were equally disturbed by British investor's "significant role" in the bank's operation. (Volkomer, Walter E., American Government, 6th Ed., pp 34) In direct retaliation, European bankers withdrew 7 million dollars in hard coin specie which triggered a gripping economic depression in the U.S. As if that wasn't enough punishment for turning against the Royal Crown's constituency, Great Brittan declared war on the U.S. and in 1812 invaded our soil. This war resulted in the loss of many American lives, not to mention the burning of the U.S. Capitol, the White House, Library of Congress, and several other libraries. Stamping out our history from the very start has been a commonplace method of robbing Americans of any sense of separation and freedom from foreign rule. In retrospect, this is one of the very few wars that were not followed by a period of economic growth, rather a depression. Although, that does not mean Great Brittan was opposed to bringing our freedom face to face with evil from the inside out. For example, in the case of McCulloch v Maryland, 1819, the U.S. Congress had crafted a system of national banks through legislation. Yet, the State of Maryland imposed a tax on the banks therein for doing business (the banks however refused to comply with state law). One of the State of Maryland's chief arguments raised the question as to whether Constitution afforded power to Congress to "delegate" the creation of specie (coinage of gold and silver) to the national banks and/or legislate to create the banks as well? The state held that the banking system in its operation was therefore unconstitutional. However, not surprisingly, Chief Justice John Marshall upheld the constitutionality of the banking system, nonetheless. (Volkomer, Walter E., American Government, 6th Ed., pp 48-49) It is not hard to fathom why the Lord raised his prophet, Joseph Smith, Jr. during this time and through whom he organized his church with a mere 6 members in 1830. In 1832, (4 years early) the Second National Bank attempted to renew its charter (engineered by Nicholas Biddle, under the influence of Congressmen Henry Clay and Daniel Webster). However, a Constitutionalist named Andrew Jackson, then President of the United States, vetoed Congress's bill for the re-charter on the grounds that the bank's operation was unconstitutional. Regarding this matter, President

Andrew Jackson declared, "If Congress has the right under the Constitution to issue paper money, it was given them to use themselves, not to be delegated to individuals or corporations" (such as the Federal Reserve today, for example, a private foreign corporation with the power of all three branches of government). (Redemption Manual, 4th ed., pp 127) Three years later an attempt was made on Andrew Jackson's life. Astonishingly, the lone gunman carrying two pistols was unsuccessful as both weapons misfired. The assailant (Richard Lawrence, an attorney) was met with President Jackson's walking cane in response. This attempt on the President's life was no coincidence, however. Andrew Jackson truly believed "the people are the sovereigns; they can alter and amend." This was a very pro-American/anti-foreign powers bold stance to take, and emphatically true. A little background on Andrew Jackson: when young Andrew was 14 years old (1781), during the Revolutionary War, he was captured by the invading British and made a prisoner of war.

Yet, in the face of tyranny and in a pure demonstration of his will to remain sovereign himself against foreign powers rule, young Andrew Jackson once refused to shine a British officer's shoes. In consequence of his stance, he was severely punished. The officer in question cut Andrew Jackson across the hand and head, his face being permanently scared." (Volkomer, Walter E., American Government, 6th ed., pp 52, 54, 59) No wonder President Jackson's nickname was "Old Hickory." Let it be understood, there are families, royal and the like, which understood before the birth of this nation that money at its root can be used to control and manipulate the administration of the rule of law and those people who serve under its weight. In 1791, Mayer Rothchild stated: "Allow me to issue and control a nation's currency, and I care not who writes the laws." (Stormer, John A., The Death of a Nation, pp180) Thomas Jefferson well understood the ills associated with the instituting of a central bank; whereas he repeatedly warned Americans about the detriment keenly associated with such fiscal relinquishments. In 1815 he stated: "The dominion which the banking institutions have obtained over the minds of our citizens . . . must be broken, or it will break us." (Stormer, John A., The Death of a Nation, pp 180) In 1791 the U.S. National debt was at $75 million, (in 1835 our National debt was resolved, and the treasury enjoyed a surplus of $5,000 under President Andrew Jackson) today the national debt increases by $75 million on an hourly basis. (pp 181) The event that most likely sparked the fire that later culminated in a cowardly attempt on President Andrew Jackson's life (1835) occurred at a delegation of bankers in 1832, at which he addressed those in attendance: "Gentleman, I have had men watching you for a long time, and I am convinced that you have used the funds of the bank to speculate in the bread-stuffs of the country. When you won, you divided the profits amongst you, and when you lost, you charged it to the bank. You tell me that if I take the deposits from the bank and annul its charter, I shall ruin ten thousand families. That may be true, gentlemen, but that is your sin! Should I let you go on, you will ruin fifty thousand, and that would be my sin! You are a den of vipers and thieves. I intend to route you out . . . ! (pp 182) I wager that such a bold confrontation did not sit well with them, or with foreign power creditor(s). In 1774 Thomas Jefferson penned "The Rights of British America"; therein his words of warning proved prophetic for his generation and unto today's generation as well: "Single acts of tyranny may be ascribed to the accidental opinion of a day; but a series of oppressions, begun at a distinguished period and pursued unalterably through every change of ministers, too plainly prove a deliberate, systematic plan of reducing [a people] to slavery." (pp 200) Benjamin Franklin wisely proclaimed: "Those who give up essential liberty to obtain a little temporary safety, deserve neither liberty nor safety." (Stormer, John A., Death of a Nation, pp 199) Sovereignty (ultimate legal authority) in the U.S. means that the American people are the source of all legal authority. The divinely inspired writers of the Constitution For the United States of America did not agree that neither the Federal nor the States were the final or ultimate source of legal authority. In fact, there are two systems of legal authority or government functioning in the same geographic area. They are State and Federal Governments, with democratically elected representatives in each system, but in and of the same area of the U.S. It has been stated by Constitutional Scholars that dual government "was precisely what American Federalism provided for, the doctrine of Popular Sovereignty made it possible."

With respect to National Supremacy (the U.S. Constitution, all federal laws, and treaties are superior to conflicting provisions of the state constitutions and laws), Article VI of the Constitution declares: "This Constitution, and the Laws of the United States which shall be made in Pursuance thereof; and all Treaties made, or which shall be made, under the Authority of the United States, shall be supreme law of the land; and the judges in every state shall be bound thereby, any Thing in the Constitution or Laws of any State to the Contrary notwithstanding." (Volkomer, Walter E., American Government, 6th Ed., pp 38) It is up to every American and freedom loving people to approximate themselves away from those who would rather shackle us with such un-payable burdens through the use of writing ordinances, statutes, codes, rules, and other fictions into law in order to contractually enslave the people they adamantly claim to serve; yet they do no great service to which said debtors, otherwise informed, knowingly would accept as their representatives in such a democracy.

II

A Grim Revelation

On December 25, 1832 (as is recorded in the Doctrine and Covenants 38: 25-30; 45: 63; 42: 64; and 87: 1-6, 8) Joseph Smith, Jr. received a revelation from the Lord regarding a future event that would change the American landscape, which would plague our nation. The prophet Joseph explained that there would be a war between the northern and southern states, the Civil War!

The aforementioned references compiled are as follows: "I say unto you that the enemy in the secret chambers seeketh your lives. Ye hear of wars in far countries, and you say that there will soon be great wars in far countries, but ye know not the hearts of men in your own land. I tell you these things because of your prayers . . . ye hear of wars in foreign lands; but behold, I say unto you, they are nigh, even at your doors, and not many years hence ye shall hear of wars in your own lands . . . Let him that goeth to the east teach them that shall be converted to flee to the west, and this in consequence of that which is coming on the earth, and of secret combinations . . . Verily, thus saith the Lord concerning the wars that will shortly come to pass, beginning at the rebellion of South Carolina, which will eventually terminate in the death and misery of many souls; And the time will come that war will be poured out upon all nations, beginning at this place. For behold, the Southern States shall be divided against the

Northern States, and the Southern States will call on other nations, even the nation of Great Brittan, as it is called, and they shall also call upon other nations, in order to defend themselves against other nations; and then war shall be poured out upon all nations. And it shall come to pass, after many days, slaves shall rise up against their masters, who shall be marshaled and disciplined for war. And it shall come to pass also that the remnants who are left of the land will marshal themselves, and shall become exceedingly angry, and shall vex the Gentiles with a sore vexation. And thus, with the sword and by bloodshed the inhabitants of the earth shall mourn . . . Wherefore, stand ye in holy places, and be not moved." In 1832, the same year the prophet Joseph Smith received the aforementioned revelation, President Andrew Jackson, after denying the early re-charter of the 2nd National Bank (a foreign controlled central bank) due to its Unconstitutional premise for operation, ordered his appointed Secretary of The U.S. Treasury, Roger B. Taney (a strong opponent to corporate privilege) to withdraw the government's gold and silver from the national bank and deposit such into state financial institutions called "pet banks". This was the first time a President of the United States claimed victory at polls allowed him to act independently of Congress. (Redemption Manual, 4th Ed., pp 324).

From a historical armchair it is understandable to ascertain why the Lord would have revealed such to Joseph Smith, Jr., then to the Saints for their own future preparations to make their way west, out of the line of fire so that the church as a whole may endure. Otherwise, in the Eastern States (North or South) the environment for the church's survival would have been too perilous to risk in open war for, or against either side. Furthermore, with President Andrew Jackson and his constituencies' stance to uphold the Constitution For the United States of America, despite Congress and the foreign powers creditor(s), the stage was being set for Rome and Great Brittan's retaliatory act of vengeance for such treachery in their Monarchical, Papal faces. Such measures did not begin, however, with the Civil War's beginning. Joseph Smith, Jr., also adamantly upheld the Constitution and stood boldly for its inherently inspired design at its inception. He received the following revelation from the Lord regarding its intended purpose, in Doctrine and Covenants 101: 78-80, we read:

> *"That every man may act in doctrine and principle pertaining to futurity, according to moral agency which I have given unto him, that every man may be accountable for his own sins in the day of judgment. Therefore, it is not right that any man should be in bondage one to another. And for this purpose, have I established the Constitution of this land, by the hands of wise men whom I raised up unto this very purpose . . ."*

History is burdened with evidence of the fact that there were those who would thwart the Constitution and planned its very destruction. In fact, despite the war of 1812, a national archivist named David Dodge discovered a book named 2 VA LAW in the Library of Congress. Dodge later revealed, "This is an un-catalogued book in the rare book section that reveals a plan to overthrow the Constitution by secret agreements engineered by lawyers of the time." (Redemption Manual, 4th Ed., pp 126)

Those secret agreements are still in force today; whereas there are those who vehemently work to counterfeit Constitutional law with something less durable, more pliable, in order to construe and construct, in essence, to manipulate the vast majority of cases (Federal, State and Local) to benefit lawmakers themselves (a wealthy minority group). Such lesser testaments are a fallacy of words disguised as lawful, hidden under fictional terms such as legal, legislative, addendum and amendment, then "sold" to the American populous as if it were wholly their idea, as well as a benefit collectively; though, these are merely tactful ways of more fully, contractually enslaving the minds of men. Zachary Taylor, our 12th President (1849- 1850) made the following declaration: "For more than a half century, during which Kingdoms and empires have fallen, this Union has stood unshaken. The patriots who formed it have long since descended to the grave; yet it still remains the proudest monument to their memory." (Volkomer, Walter E., American Government, 6th Ed., pp 84) President Taylor's service as Commander-in-Chief was short-lived however, whereas he died suddenly in 1850. The doctors of the time diagnosed the cause of death being gastroenteritis, or inflammation of the stomach and intestines. This sudden death gave rise to certain speculation that President Taylor had been poisoned, and the use of arsenic was thought to of been induced, in particular. What could be cause for such a conspiracy? A motive to consider could be a derivative of President Taylor's convictions to oppose the plans of influential Southerners who were pushing for succession from the Union. In fact, in a meeting with Southern States leaders, between February and March of 1850, regarding this topic of succession, President Taylor succinctly warned that anyone "taken in rebellion against the Union" . . . will be hanged. (Volkomer, Walter E., American Government, 6th Ed., pp 153, 156) To the Southerners of the time those were fighting words! President Taylor further acknowledged that for any State(s) who chose succession, he would lead the Federal Army against them personally. It could be stated, in theory, if Zachary Taylor's death was a result of actions taken by Southern States leaders who wanted succession, the Civil War actually began at the moment of the President's fateful demise. President George Washington warned against blind party loyalty in his farewell speech, wholeheartedly akin to what preceded the aforementioned American conflict: "The common and continual mischiefs of the spirit of party are sufficient to make it the interest and duty of a wise people to discourage and restrain it. It serves always to distract the public councils and enfeeble the public administration. It agitates the community with ill-founded jealousies and false alarms; kindles the animosity of one party against another; foments occasionally riot and insurrection . . . A fire not to be quenched, it demands a uniform vigilance to prevent its bursting into a flame, lest, instead of warming, it should consume." (Beck, Glenn, Glenn Beck's Common Sense, pp 59) His words too, were prophetic; wherefore, it was due to a divisionary barrage of political diatribe, at least in part, men, women, and families died by the tens of thousands in the great and terrible Civil War! Twenty-five years following the attempt on Andrew Jackson's life the Civil War officially began with an act of Congress. Whereas, in "1860-1861 the (British controlled) Southern States walked out of the United States Congress assembled. This created "sine die" (without day), a situation in which not enough representatives were present to carry on legislative business." The newly elected, very wealthy President Abraham Lincoln, a lawyer and noble esquire, was left to resolve this crisis. At the moment of "sine die" the United States of America, the social compact known as the Constitution For the United States of America was lost, null and void.

Thus, the country formerly known as the United States of America ceased to exist. (Redemption Manual, 4th Ed., pp 123) In response to this dire state of emergency, President Lincoln enacted the very first Executive Order in American history, namely Lincoln Executive Proclamation 1, April 15, 1861. It is readily known and can be aptly proven that the United States "have been ruled since this time by these same Military Executive

Powers denoted as Executive Orders" (Martial Rule due to a Presidential Declaration of National Emergency). (Redemption Manual, 4th Ed., pp 128) What is martial rule or martial law? The Preamble of the Expatriation Act of 1868 states: "Under martial law, title is a mere fiction, since all property belongs to the military except for that property which the Commander-in-Chief may, in his benevolence, exempt from taxation and seizure and upon which he allows the 'enemy' (Americans) to reside." Yet, another opportunity and challenge the Civil War's political atmosphere set the stage for was the Trading with the Enemy Act, which passed under Executive Order by President Lincoln. In stark contrast, President Lincoln sounded a different bell of alarm in a message to Congress, December 3, 1861:

"No men living are more worthy to be trusted than those who toil up from poverty—none less inclined to take or touch aught which they have not honestly earned, let them beware of surrendering a political power which they already possess (Sovereignty), and which if surrendered, will surely be used to close the door of advancement against such as they, and to fix new disabilities and burdens upon them, till all of liberty shall be lost." (Redemption Manual, 4th Ed., pp 130) Today, when we contract with the government for licensure, for financial benefits, for loans, surrendering our STRAWMAN name, using our social security identification number, for example, we are in fact contracting with, and surrendering to the U.S. Government, whose jurisdiction only lies within the boundaries of the 10 square miles located in the District of Columbia, and thereafter we become captive, subject to their agents (Local, State and Federal Law Enforcers: CIA, FBI, DHS, BATF, NSA, Secret Service), debtors to their collectors (IRS, Department of the U.S. Treasury, and Federal Reserve). On February 21, 1871 the forty-first Congress of the United States ratified the Act to

Provide a Government for the District of Columbia, in Section 34, the 3rd Session, Chapters 61 and 62, the following true proclamation came to light: "THE UNITED STATES OF AMERICA is a corporation, whose jurisdiction is applicable only in the ten-mile-square parcel of land known as the District of Columbia and to whatever properties are legally titled to the UNITED STATES, by its registration in the corporate County, State, and Federal governments that are under military power of the UNITED STATES and its creditors." This piece of legislation is further reiterated in the UNITED STATES CODE, Title 28, 3002 (15) (3): "That all departments of the UNITED STATES CORPORATION are part of the corporation. Title 28, UNITED STATES CODE, is Copyrighted, per Private International Law. Indeed, the UNITED STATES CODE, in its entirety, is Copyrighted Private International Law, and applicable only in the District of Columbia." (Redemption Manual, 4th Ed., pp 134) This legislation of 1871 was able to come forth only after a representative like President Lincoln no longer held veto power, because he was martyred, assassinated, because he was dead. President Lincoln, with respect to the direct influence of the Jesuit agents of the Catholic Church in Rome (a creditor) on the Civil War, stated the following: "This war would never have been possible without the sinister influence of the Jesuits. We owe it to popery that we now see our land reddened with the blood of her noblest sons . . . I pity the priests, the bishops, and the monks of Rome in the United States when the people realize that they are, in great part, responsible for the tears and bloodshed in this war." (Ibid. pp 296, 297—

Hughes, Bill, The Secret Terrorists, pp 55) Despite the challenges of the Civil War and those foreign forces which secretly combined to see it through to get control of the money (people, resources, property, and specie), President Lincoln takes his life into his own hands when he declares a new monetary policy for America: "The Government should create, issue, and circulate all the currency and credits needed to satisfy the spending power of consumers. By the adoption of these principles, the taxpayers will be saved immense sums of interest (which is what taxes are mainly used to pay for, the interest on our national debt to the foreign power creditors). Money will cease to be master and become the servant of humanity . . . the privilege of creating and issuing money is not only the supreme prerogative of government, but it is the government's greatest opportunity." (Redemption Manual, 4th Ed., pp 130) Lincoln was offering all peoples of the United States freedom from foreign powers rule and control, sovereignty all their own, to become agents unto themselves, no longer subjects and debtors. These aforementioned fiscal principles boldly proclaimed by President Lincoln would have revitalized the world economy if implemented. However, before President Abraham Lincoln could successfully organize the Southern States governing bodies, effectively rescind the Executive Orders of Martial Rule due to a National Emergency, and finally put into practice his monetary plan he was assassinated (only 3 weeks following the announcement of his proposed fiscal policy to Congress). As a result, the government in this country continued thenceforth unto this very day to "operate fully under the authority of private international law dictated by the creditor." (Redemption Manual, 4th Ed., pp 130) President James A. Garfield was an adamant proponent of a conservative fiscal policy, who openly urged the payment of government debts resume using specie.

An excerpt from his inaugural address of 1881 reads, "Whoever controls the volume of money in any country is absolute master of all industry and commerce . . . The chief duty of the National Government in connection with the currency of the country is to coin money and declare its value.

Grave doubts have been entertained whether Congress is authorized by the Constitution to make any form of paper money legal tender. The present issue of the United States notes has been sustained by the necessities of war; but such paper should depend for its value and currency upon its convenience in use and its prompt redemption in coin at the will of the holder, and not upon its compulsory circulation. These notes are not money but promises to pay money. If the holders (American Populous) demand it, the promise should be kept." (Redemption Manual, 4th Ed., pp 136) 200 Days later, President Garfield was shot by an Attorney and died as a result of the fatal wound 80 days thereafter. Now, to understand the influence and power, the mantel of what it meant to be an Esquire, Lawyer, and Attorney in 1881, for example, we should consider with whom their primary allegiances lie during this era of history. All attorneys, even to this very day, are certified as lawyers by the IBA (International Bar Association), which was originally chartered by the King of England, known as the BAR (British Accreditation Registry). Furthermore, all certified attorneys are given a title of nobility, namely Esquire. The BAR is headquartered in London, England; wherefore, all attorney's primary allegiance, then (1881) and now, lies with the Royal Crown of England, and thereafter the U.S. Government. The U.S. Constitution, however, forbids the granting and holding of titles of nobility on American soil, as we read in Article I, Section 9: "No Title of Nobility shall be granted by the United States: And no Person holding any office of Profit or Trust under them, shall, without the Consent of Congress, accept of any present, Emolument, Office, or

Title, of any kind whatever, from any King, Prince, or foreign state." (Mcguire, Robert A., To Form A More Perfect Union, pp 232) Coincidentally, should the President, members of Congress, or members of the Supreme Court commit

"Treason, Bribery, or other High Crimes" they could be subject to Impeachment and if convicted be removed from office, be subject to fines and/or a prison sentence. However, only one Supreme Court Justice has ever been impeached (Samuel Chase in 1805), but not one member of the Supreme Court has ever been removed from office. Hence, the power of the BAR to protect those ultimately loyal to the interests of the Royal Crown of England in this country, and to provide certain immunities. This is in spite of The U.S. Constitution, Article I, Section 3, which states: "Judgment in cases of Impeachment shall not extend further than to removal from office, and disqualification to hold and enjoy any office of Honor, Trust, or Profit under the United States: but the Party convicted shall nevertheless be liable and subject to Indictment, Trial, Judgment and Punishment, according to the Law." (McGuire, Robert A., To Form A More Perfect Union, pp 229) It is important to note that the Declaration of Independence, on July 4, 1776, contains several claims for redress against the Royal Crown of England, King George III, wherein it is declared: ""He has combined with others to subject us to a jurisdiction foreign to our constitution, and unacknowledged by our laws giving his assent to their acts of pretended legislation." (Volkomer, Walter E.,

American Government, 6th Ed., pp 351) This same redress applies today with greater fervor than it ever did then. Following the assassination of President Garfield in 1881, Chester Alan Arthur was sworn in as our 21rst President of the United States (1881-1885). One of his famous quotes gives a little picture into his stance on transparency: "I may be President of the United States, but my private life is nobody's damned business!" (Smith, Carter, Smithsonian Presidents, pp 132) Is it a coincidence that on May 13, 1884, under President Arthur's administration, Congress officially repealed the 1862 Test Oath which was originally written into law in order to mandate that all holders of office take an oath to affirm they have never participated in illegal or disloyal conduct? (Smith, Carter, Smithsonian Presidents, pp 134) Rather, the converse is true, it is of no small coincidence at all. As we move on into the 20th Century, let us consider first the men and women who in the latter gave the last full measure their devotion in service to our great land, in search of freedom they perhaps never came to know in this life. Penned from a book called "America Through British Eyes", an excerpt from the section: America in 1905: "Business is King", the following observation came to light: "In the United States, business, that is to say, industry, commerce, and finance . . . dwarf all other interests, all other occupations . . . Business is King . . . Working men follow, though hitherto with unequal steps, the efforts at combination which the lords of production and distribution have been making. The consumer stands . . . with no clear view of the steps he may make for his own protection. Now, it is the power of wealth which enables the few to combine so as to gain command of the sources of wealth . . . Americans have been the most individualistic of peoples that they are now the people among whom the art of combination has reached its maximum? . . . Wealth, gathered into a small number of hands, . . . dominate even the enormous market of America." (America's History, 5th Ed., pp 594)

Those who stand in government, or in other special places of authority, who dare stand up to the Money Kings, historically, find that their life's march towards death comes at a much more abrupt and rapid pace. Another distinct example of a real American hero for independence is demonstrated when one considers the events that led up to the assassination of President William McKinley, our 25th President (1897-1901), and the cowardice of the Money Kings. President McKinley ran for office using a pro-tariff, pro-gold standard campaign stance. On March 4,

1897, McKinley is inaugurated as President of the United States of America. 11 days later, March 15, 1897, McKinley calls for a special session of Congress to revise Tariff laws. The result of which is in July of 1897, following President McKinley signing the new bill (Dingley Tariff Law), which raises tariffs by 57%, resulted in significant price spikes in goods. Then, in an effort to comply with the other side of the coin he campaigned on, President McKinley, on March 7, 1900, signs the Gold Standard Act into law, making gold the standard value for all money in America (this would cause any central bank with its money being backed by something of lesser value to bankrupt, ultimately). Then, on March 11, 1901, Great Brittan informs the U.S. that "it rejects our amendments to the Hay-Pauncefort Treaty, enacted by the Senate, with respect to a Central American canal. Then, on September 6, 1901, President William McKinley is assassinated, shot by a "loan gunman" named Leon Czolgoz, a Polish American and supposed Anarchist.

Thereafter, President Theodore Roosevelt was sworn in, and Brittan thereafter decides to change its mind about the Hay-Pauncefort Treaty and supports the U.S.'s designs for a Central American canal. If the British had any quarrel with President McKinley, it was over the question of the Gold Standard in America, and perhaps the tariffs, but not the canal. President Theodore Roosevelt once stated, "A man who has never gone to school may steal from a freight car, but if he has a university

education, he may steal the whole railroad." Ironically, on June 29, 1906, Roosevelt signs into law the Hepburn Act, revitalizing the Interstate Commerce Commission, which greatly expanded governmental authority over the railroad system throughout the U.S.

Then, in March of 1907 there was a stock market crash causing a panic due to the unavailability of currency which was primarily controlled by foreign powers creditors. However, J.P. Morgan and Company intervened in December of that year and the panic ends! It is also imperative to note that on October 23, 1907, President Theodore Roosevelt, following his subsequent return from a "hunting trip", allowed J.P. Morgan and Company to purchase the Tennessee Iron and Coal Company, free of any liability or exposure to an inherent anti-trust lawsuit from the federal government. How did J.P. Morgan and Company afford to make such purchases only 6 weeks following his installments of massive amounts of money into a fund bailing out the United States Government, in fact saving them from our creditors? We will soon have to take a closer look at the Company of friends so invested with J.P. Morgan at the time to comprehend such an undertaking. Then, on March 30, 1908, Congress passes the Aldrich—Vreeland Act, allowing national banks to issue money based on commercial paper and government bonds. The act in question also allowed for the creation of the National Monetary Council (predecessor to the Federal Reserve Act of 1913). Also, under President Roosevelt, U.S. Representatives support and promote the creation of a World Court, on June 15, 1907, at the 2nd International Peace Conference in the Hague. (Volkomer, Walter E., American Government, 6th Ed., pp 153, 156, 161, and 163)

These Money Kings from afar invaded our home of the brave long ago, and have since, by coercion, in secret, taken possession of the whole of it! If this were not the case, can it be that there is any form of property ownership readily available to the American populous upon which a tax, tariff, or other government related charges of usury are not placed prior to it coming into the hands of the consumer, and in many cases as it is being otherwise relinquished elsewhere as well? Furthermore, in large measure, unto what do these consumer costs go to? One expensive, expansive example is that from 1890 to 1917 the number of government employees increased from roughly 170,000 to 520,000. (America's History, 5th Ed., pp 600) This dramatic growth occurred primarily during President Woodrow Wilson's first term of office (elected in 1912). The taxes are used to pay the interest on the un-payable debt incurred by our government, owed to the foreign powers creditor(s). The budget for expansion grows because those who decide for us (democratically elected officials) apply for and secure additional loans against our good name in the world, the labor of the people, citizenry (indentured servitude, slavery, debtorship). Several legislative changes occurred under the influence of the "Money Kings" and we will discuss at length how this came about and what effect it had upon our nation then and now.

III

Money At The Root

In 1909, default loomed over the U.S. once again. The U.S. Government asked the Crown of England, our creditor, for an extension of time to pay down the loan. Our then creditor granted our Government a twenty-year extension on the loan in question (do the math—1929 and the Great Depression). In 1910, Seven prominent gentlemen met in secret on Jeckyll Island, Georgia to plan, to concoct, to conceive of a bill that would later be known as the Federal Reserve Act. The actual founders of the Federal Reserve, the gentlemen in question, are as follows: Nelson Aldrich (Chairman of the National Monetary Commission, a J.P. Morgan business associate, and father-in-law to John D. Rockefeller, Jr.; Benjamin Strong (head of J.P. Morgan's Bankers Trust Company); Charles D. Norton (the President of J.P. Morgan's First National Bank of New York); Henry P. Davison (Senior partner of the J.P. Morgan Company); Abraham Piatt Andrew (Assistant Secretary of the United States Treasury); Frank A. Vanderlip (National City Bank of New York President—the most powerful bank in the U.S. at the time, also representing William Rockefeller and Kuhn, Loeb & Company—an international banking house); and finally, "the father of the Federal Reserve Plan", Mr. Paul Warburg (partner in Kuhn, Loeb & Company, representing the Rothchild banking dynasty of both France and England—brother to the same Max Warburg who then was at the head of the Warburg Banking Consortium in the Netherlands and Germany). (Redemption Manual, 4th Ed., pp 168) President Theodore

Roosevelt, in a debate against the challenger for the Presidency, Woodrow

Wilson, in October of 1912 stated: "This is a struggle for emancipation (from foreign power creditors). If America is not to have free enterprise, then she can have freedom of no sort whatsoever." (America's History, 5th Ed., pp 598) The February 9, 1935, issue of the Saturday Evening Post reported a statement by Mr. Frank Vanderlip, co-author to the Federal Reserve Act of 1913, speaking to the secret way in which he and his co-conspirators, at the aforementioned Jeckyll Island meeting, founded its creation. He revealed, "There was an occasion, near the close of 1910, when I was as secretive, as furtive . . . as any conspirator . . . I do not feel it is any exaggeration to speak of our secret expedition to Jeckyll Island as the occasion of the actual conception of what eventually became the Federal Reserve System . . .

If it were to be exposed publicly that our particular group had gotten together and written a banking bill, that bill would have no chance whatever of passage by Congress . . . As with all Cartels, it had to be created by legislation and sustained by the power of government under the deception of protecting the consumer." (Volkomer, Walter E., American Government, 6 Ed., pp 169).

With respect to the Federal Reserve System, the Rothchild Brothers had this to say regarding its creation: "The few who can understand the system (check money and credits) will either be so interested in its profits, or so dependent on its favors, that there will be no opposition from that class, while on the other hand, the great body of the people mentally incapable of comprehending the tremendous advantage that capital derives from the system, will bear its burdens without complaint, and perhaps without even suspecting that the system is inimical to their interests." (Volkomer, Walter E., America's History, 6th Ed., pp 170) Thomas Woodrow Wilson, our 28th President (1913-1921), signed the Federal Reserve Act of 1913 into law. President Wilson is famously remembered as stating, quote: "It is not men that interest or disturb me primarily; it is ideas. Ideas live; men die." (Smith, Carter, Smithsonian Presidents, pp 172, 174) The Federal Reserve System "idea" resulted in the financialization of our great nation. What is financialization? It is readily defined as: "a process whereby financial services, broadly construed, take over the dominant economic, cultural, and political role in a national economy." (Phillips, Kevin, American Theocracy, pp 268) What is the Federal Reserve? "The Federal Reserve is a private bank who is acting fiscal agent of the creditor for the Crown of England as the Exchequer of the Vatican to service the federal military government construct's un-payable debt." (Redemption Manual, 4th Ed., pp 161) Furthermore, the Rothchild dynasty "holds the key to the wealth of the Catholic Church of the Vatican", the same international family, a financial consortium behemoth, who participated in the co-conspiracy to manipulate Congress and the President to propose and ratify legislation designed to control the creation of currency, which indirectly heavily influences the economy, commerce, government, and lawmaking, all for their own financial gain, at the expense of the vast majority of Americans. Douglas Rushkoff, in his inciteful book "Life Inc." explains the operation of a central bank: "Our money— dollars, pounds, euros, yen and all of those other currencies we can get at the airport exchange or invest in at the ForEx.com—is lent into existence by a central bank. This bank is usually a private corporation chartered by the government to manage currency. The corporation—be it the Bank of

England or the Federal Reserve—lends a certain amount of money to a smaller bank, which then lends it to a company or person . . . The agenda of central currency—the bias of this medium—is to promote competition, require the expansion of the economy, and increase overall indebtedness to the central bank. Central currency favors central authority, because it is created by a central, chartered monopoly, with the provision that it be paid back to the central bank, with interest. Those on the periphery owe, while those in the center grow. This, in turn, leads to the redistribution of wealth away from those who actually do work and towards the lending classes." (Rushkoff, Douglas, Life Inc., pp 162-163)

Unto what extent does the Vatican's influence have on government, on economies, and on world policy making? Let us consider a quote from an article found in the Western Watchman, by one Priest Phelan, dated June 27, 1912: "Why if the government of the United States were at war with the Church, we would say tomorrow, to hell with the Government of the United States; and if the Church and all of the Governments of the world were at war, we would say: To hell with all of the Governments of the world. Why is it that the Pope has so much power? Why the Pope is the ruler of the world. All emperors, all the kings, all the princes, all the presidents of the world are as these ALTAR BOYS of mine." (Hughes, Bill, The Secret Terrorists, pp 22) Napoleon Bonaparte had this to say with respect to the Jesuit Order of the Catholic Church: "The Jesuits are a military organization, not a religious order. Their chief is a general of an army, not the mere father abbot of a monastery. And the aim of this organization is: POWER. Power in its most despotic exercise. Absolute power, universal power, power to control the world by the volition of a single man. Jesuitism is the most absolute of despotisms; and at the same time the greatest and most enormous of abuses . . . The general of the Jesuits insists on being master, Sovereign, over the Sovereign. Wherever the Jesuits are admitted they will be masters, cost what it may. Their society is by nature dictatorial, and therefore it is the irreconcilable enemy of all constituted authority (enemy of the Constitution and Sovereign People). Every act, every crime, however atrocious, is a meritorious work, if committed for the interest of the society of Jesuits, or by the order of the general." (Hughes, Bill, The Secret Terrorists, pp 13) The monarchies of Rome and England along with its constituent banking houses and agents who operate in secret, combined to create a network of central banks and collection agencies . . . a cartel which would be the model for every future aspiring secret combination that would manifest themselves in the everyday lives of the common man then and now.

IV

The Great and Terrible Depression

With respect to the "wickedness of monopolies" in the United States, the author John Kenneth Galbraith, in his book "The New Industrial State" explains the justification behind the passage of the Sherman Act and creation of the of the FTC (Federal Trade Commission). He asserts that the Sherman Act prohibited combinations in restraint of trade and made it a misdemeanor to "monopolize" or "attempt to monopolize" any interstate or foreign commerce. Though, the Clayton and Federal Trade Commission Acts of the early Wilson Administration extended the prohibition to particular steps—price discrimination, exclusive contracts, acquisition of stock in a competing corporation, undefined fairness—which might lessen competition. And legislation following WWII—The Celler-Kefauver Antimerger Act—proscribed mergers between firms which might promote monopoly." (Galbraith, Kenneth, The New Industrial State, pp 169) Woodrow Wilson, the incumbent President in 1916, ran for his second term on the platform of "He kept of out of the War!" President Wilson created a committee of publicity charged with pontificating a campaign of persuasion and hired both Edward Bernays and George Creel to run it. The slogan of the committee was "to make the world safe for democracy." This committee eventually became the Committee on Public Information, or CPI. The CPI, under the auspices of the Espionage Act of 1917 and the Sedition Act of 1918 were in effect silencing newspapers who criticized the war (WWI) effort; and in turn, utilizing the media outlets to play on the populous' emotions regarding the possibility of German attacks upon U.S. soil, an invasion. In 1921, Rodger Babson, a business theorist and statistician observed in retrospect, "The war taught us the power of propaganda. Now when we have anything to sell the American people, we will know how to sell it." (Rushkoff, Douglas, Life Inc., pp 104) The overall theme for the travesty we call the Great Depression could be found, if you will, in Proverbs 22, comprising verses 7, 16, 22-23 and 26-27: "The rich (monarchies, lending class, central banks) ruleth over the poor, and the borrower (citizen in good standing) is servant to the lender. He that oppresseth (IRS and Secret Service) the poor to increase his riches, and he (U.S. Government) that giveth to the rich (foreign powers creditors), shall surely come to want (national debt). For the Lord will plead their (debtor citizen) cause and spoil the souls of them that spoiled them. Be not thou one of them that strike hands (contracting with government agencies for temporary financial gain, leading to long term indebtedness), or of them that are sureties for debts (debtor citizen = modern day slavery). If thou hast nothing to pay (get out of debt, stay out of debt), why should he take away thy bed from under thee?" Too many citizens were overburdened with debt.

The U.S. Government being the corporate group of democratically elected officials enriching themselves with power, influence, and money through a budgetary process of going into debt with the foreign power creditors in order to expand government; then instituting a multi-tiered taxation of citizenry and exercising additional government controls over

their potential for financial independence through fictional lawmaking. Then, publicly branding their conviluded legislative writs of oppression constitutional and lawful. With a narrow view of government's role, in conjunction with their foreign corporate partners (bosses) just prior to the Great Depression, let's remember that in 1909 the U.S. Government was

granted a 20-year extension on our national debt. In 1929, due to our government officials' desire to benefit the lending class and to enslave and win the hearts and minds of the poorer classes; moreover, to convince them of the ever-increasing need for government's role in their lives, when the foreign lender(s) called in their debts the U.S. Government had to make every concession possible—to deal in order to avoid being otherwise dealt with; even if it meant sacrificing so much that was great about our country in the terrible process. The following quote will shed light on why the Great Depression(s) happen and will yet happen in this country, and throughout the world: "By a continuing process of inflation, governments can confiscate secretly and unobserved, an important part of the wealth of its citizens. There is no subtler, no surer means of overturning the existing basis of society than to debauch the currency. The process engages all the hidden forces of economic law on the side of destruction and does it in such a manner which not one man in a minion is able to diagnose." (Redemption Manual, 4th Ed., pp 73) Before discussing in fact the events that culminated in the Great Depression in History, let us consider the heart, the mind and spirit of the Monarchs, along with their constituent lending class, who called in their debt to our government sparking the fires of economic flames in this country, which consumed so many in its wake. A revealing quote from the Civil Servants Yearbook, "The Organizer", the January of 1934 edition, delineates the clear intentions of the international bankers for the creation of a central bank, and what is therein called "The Bankers Manifesto", it reads as follows: "Capital must protect itself in every way, through combination and through legislation. Debts must be collected, and loans and mortgages foreclosed as soon as possible. When, through a process of law the common people have lost their homes, they will be more tractable and more easily governed by the strong arm of the law, applied by the central power of wealth, under control of leading financiers. People without homes will not quarrel with their leaders. This is well known among our principal men now engaged in forming an imperialism of capital to govern the world. By dividing the people, we can get them to expend their energies in fighting over questions of no importance to us except as teachers of the common herd. Thus, by discreet action we can secure for ourselves what has been generally planned and successfully accomplished." (Redemption Manual, 4th Ed., pp 188)

The aforementioned happened, through the conquest of war and debauching of currency, in the land of Germany. In 1919, Germany's Mark was worth about 25 cents (U.S.); however, following WWI and the subsequent destruction of the German economy along with its supply of gold reserves, the Mark, within four years from that time fell to a cataclysmic value of four trillion when compared with the value of one U.S. Dollar's buying power. A Reader's Digest article explained further:

"The German middle classes had lost all their savings. The value of every pension was wiped out. All securities were gone. Then the people were ready to listen to any demagogue who would voice their bitterness:

his name was Adolf Hitler." (Stormer, John A., Death of A Nation, pp 15-16) There was a demagogue in our country whose representation was no less fierce, or destructive than the aforementioned fascist. He would become our nation's first actual dictator, the 4 term President, Franklin Delano Roosevelt. He was President on Black Tuesday, Black Thursday and every other dark day in America that followed for years and years to come. Wherefore, "The Great Depression reduced personal savings from $4.2 billion in 1929 to a net dissaving of $900 million in 1933 and gross business savings from $11.2 billion to $3.2billion." (Galbraith, John Kenneth, The New Industrial State, pp 205)

Taken from an excerpt found in "America's History, 5th Edition", additional factoids shed light on what the majority of Americans were impacted with in one way or another, collectively: On "Black Thursday", October 24, 1929, the stock market took the first hit bursting the bubble of growth which had steadily progressed as such in the U.S. since 1921; as stock prices since that time to 1929 had risen 40%. But on October 24 and again in October 29, "Black Tuesday", more than $28 million in shares changed hands due to the initial panic. Overnight, stock values fell from $87 billion to $55 billion. The market, which to 8 years or better, previously reflecting 40% in growth, now was on a one-way-non-stop freight train to hell! The U.S. GDP was cut nearly in half from 1929 to 1932 (from $103.1 billion to $58 billion). "Consumption expenditures dropped by 18%; construction by 78%; private investment by 88%; farm income cut in half; 9,000 banks failed, and 100,000 businesses failed. The Consumer Price Index declined by 25% and Corporate profits fell from 10 billion to 1 billion." On about October 23, 1929, unemployment was roughly 3.2%. By 1932, following the stock market crash, unemployment rose to an astonishing 24.9% (sound familiar, Greece?—25% unemployment in 2012). (America's History, 5th Ed., pp 696, 699)

Now that the American populous were in a tractable position, broken in large measure, if you will, by government and their masters of money, we can see how war could be on the horizon; but how it would play out is beyond what history has dared to record in full, because of our Government's initial quiet role of support (playing both sides) in it. In fact, war had already been declared on the American people, as well as on several other nations simultaneously and has been ever since Woodrow Wilson, then FDR came into power, especially. In 1930 "the international bankers declared several nations bankrupt, including the United States." (Redemption Manual, 4th Ed., pp 138) This was the calm before the storm erupted.

V

The Calm Before The Storm

Lenin once stated, "The surest way to overthrow an existing social order is to debauch the currency." A guide for Communists, if you will, was written by Lenin in 1902, which eludes to the following instructions: "We must go among all classes of people as their theoriticians, as propagandists, as agitators and as organizers . . . The principal thing, of course, is propaganda and agitation among all strata of people." (Stormer, John A., The Death of A Nation, pp 16, 25)

These two methods, debauching currency and organizing people in order to cause divisions, are the calm before the storm of war. The divisions in question are Communism versus Facism, either one or the other has the support of all classes, be it directly or indirectly. These two groups alone are at the heart of every political debate, every law, however uncommon, and unconstitutional. General Douglas McArthur once commented regarding the demise of any nation, moral or otherwise, with the following: "History fails to record a single precedent in which nations subject to moral decay have not passed into political and economic decline. There has been either a spiritual awakening to overcome the moral lapse, or a progressive deterioration leading to ultimate national disaster."

(Stormer, John A., Death of A Nation, pp 23) The storm I wish to speak of largely had its official beginning here in the U.S. with the creation, through legislation, of secret service institutions. For example, in 1917 Congress passed a revision to Lincoln's Trading with the Enemy Act, broadening its scope. That same year, in fact, the Department of Justice created a Bureau of Investigation (BI, predecessor to the FBI). The Bureau's name was initially the American Protective League, or APL. In July of 1917, John Herbert Hoover was hired on as a new agent therein. Less than two months later, one of the worst series of atrocious infringements upon the private lives of Americans began, it was a quiet war declared on the people of this great nation. It was a war against the civil liberties of U.S. Citizens, all in the name of protecting Americans and WWI, the war to end all wars. During September of 1917, a series of raids began on citizens living within the borders of the U.S., purportedly in hopes of discovering and/or rooting out German spies on our soil.

The two individuals mostly responsible for masterminding these violations were U.S. Attorney General, Thomas Gregory and Secretary of War, Newton D. Baker. Following these raids, the Attorney General began receiving numerous complaints which charged the APL agents with "illegal arrests, strikebreaking, wiretapping, bugging, frame-ups, extortion, blackmail, kidnappings, rapes, and in the case of Mr. Frank Little (a WWI Organizer who was kidnapped and then lynched by the APL), murder." Yet ironically not one German spy was ever caught as a result of these raids. The "BI Director Chief Bielaski . . . in his final report, claimed that out of 50,000 arrested, 1,505 had been inducted into military service and 15,000 referred to their draft boards. However, one of his assistants injudiciously admitted that out every 200 arrests, 199 were clearly mistakes." This "quiet war" was J. Edgar Hoover's first impression of how an investigative agency of government could unlawfully oppress the populous of America and escape the penalty of law, because they were immune. (Gentry, Curt, J. Edgar Hoover: The Man and The Secrets, pp 72) The duties of the secret service here in the U.S. are to "detect and arrest persons committing any offense against the laws of the United States relating to coins obligations and securities or the United States and of foreign governments; and to detect and arrest persons violating certain laws relating to the FDIC, Federal Land Banks, electronic fund transfer frauds, credit, and debit card frauds, false identification documents." (Redemption Manual, 4th Ed., pp 148) These agents, representing various agencies of government, are the army of the creditor(s) foreign to this nation. Keep this in mind as we now take a look at the legislation which came to pass under FDR's Administration, as well as support for war in foreign nations deriving therefrom. Franklin Delano Roosevelt, our 32nd President, who served four terms of office, the only president to do so, once boldly stated: "The only thing we have to fear is fear itself." With respect to FDR's leadership, one Senator Henry D. Hatfield remarked: "The country is being run by a group of college professors. This Brain Trust is endeavoring to force socialism upon the American people." (Smith, Carter, Smithsonian Presidents, pp 190, 194) FDR was innaugerated on March 4, 1933. The very next day, the 5th of March, President Roosevelt orders a Bank Holiday. Why? Since 1932, the Federal Reserve had been funneling billions of the American Citizens bank deposits in gold to Germany. Now, during this time there was a Depression-related run on all national banks for currency to be "redeemed" for specie (gold coin). However, due to the aforementioned actions of the Federal Reserve over a prolonged period sufficient specie was not available as redemption of currency, which is nothing more than a promise to pay.

This spurred the necessity for the President to make such an order official, despite the people, on behalf of the creditor(s) and their foreign constituency. Then, on April 19, 1933, FDR officially signs into law House Joint Resolution 192, taking the U.S. off of the Gold Standard once again.

Furthermore, in order to regulate Wall Street, through contract, on May 27, 1933, Congress passes the Federal Securities Act. Thus, requiring all bonds and stock issuances to be registered and approved by the Federal Government.

On June 6, 1934, FDR creates the Securities and Exchange Commission (SEC) designed to regulate, reign in and control speculation; it also served to grant licensure unto stock exchanges. Then, on June 19, 1934, Congress creates the Federal Communications Commission (FCC) which was designed to regulate all communication via radio, telegraph, and through telephone services. (Smith, Carter, Smithsonian Presidents, pp 192-196) "Big Brother" just got a lot bigger, laying the sod for the grassy knoll we as Americans live under today!

With respect to HJR 192, the 1933 legislation following the Bank Holiday aforementioned, the constitutionality of this law will forever remain in question when one considers that this law was enacted to force all American Citizens to return all gold and silver coinage to the Federal Reserve, under the auspices of a lawful edict, carrying the penalty of fines and imprisonment. This, despite Article I. Section 8 of the Constitution, which clearly states: "Congress shall have power . . . To coin money, to regulate the value thereof . . ." (America's History, Volume 1, pp D-8) As stated earlier, the Federal Reserve Bank had been funneling billions in specie to Germany, it continued even after, in 1933, one Adolf Hitler became interim Chancellor. In fact, "immense sums belonging to our national bank depositors have been given to Germany on a no collateral security whatever . . .

Billions upon Billions of our money has been pumped into Germany by the Federal Reserve Banks . . . On April 27, 1932, the Federal Reserve outfit sent $750,000, belonging to American bank depositors, in gold to Germany. A week later, another $300,000 in gold was shipped to Germany the same way. About the middle of May $12,000,000 in gold was shipped to Germany by the Federal Reserve

Banks. Almost every week there is a shipment of gold to Germany."—H.S. Kegan, The Federal Reserve Bank, The Noontide Press, 1966, pp 158 (Hughes, Bill, The Secret Terrorists, pp 74) Why was this happening? Well, Germany, following WWI was left destitute, the Mark was devalued to destruction and their infrastructure in grave

peril. The specie, robbed from the American populous through a pretended constitutional legislation enacted by Congress, signed into law by FDR, was essentially used to create Hitler's war machine! We will discuss in detail how additional resources were further allocated to Germany by prominent businessman who are celebrated household names in our country and abroad today.

On June 16, 1933, FDR signed into law the creation of the Federal Bank Deposit Insurance Corporation (FDIC), under the Banking Act of 1933. In line with our then facist position on Hitler's Germany, following the end of the Spanish Civil War, the U.S. recognizes the new Spanish Government, under the Franco dictatorship, April 1, 1939. Then, on June 28, 1940, Congress passes the Alien Registration Act, making it a crime to advocate in any way the forceful overthrow of the U.S. Government (inherently unconstitutional). Also, on September 16, 1940, FDR signs into law the Selective Training and Service Act (the Military Draft). This Act authorized the very first Peace-Time Military Draft in U.S. history. All men between the ages of 18 and 35 were required to register (contract) for military training, under penalty of law. (Smith, Carter, Smithsonian Presidents, pp 196-197) Now that some of the back doors and lower windows have been open for a candid view behind events that actually, spurred the planet into WWII, let us further consider FDR's stance regarding Hitler's blitzkrieg upon so many nations, whereas his administration stood idly by for so very long without a sincere intervention whatsoever.

On September 3, 1939, France, and England both declared war on Germany, the U.S. remains "neutral". The U.S. eventually intervenes on behalf of our "Allies" when FDR signs into law that the U.S. may send arms to whatever country it so chooses, on March 11, 1941. By this date Germany and Italy have in concert already invaded Austria (1938), Czechoslovakia (1939), Albania (1939), Poland (1939), Norway (1940), Denmark (1940) and attacked Great Brittan (1940). On May 27, 1941, Germany successfully invades and overtakes Greece and Yugoslavia. Then, on June 22, 1941, in violation of the Nazi-Soviet Non-Aggression Pact of 1939, Germany invades the Soviet Union. (Smith, Carter, Smithsonian Presidents, pp 196-198) Despite all of this aggression and
series of invasions over a period of almost 4 years against our international coalition of allies, still the U.S. remains neutral, with the only exception being arms support to Great Brittan.

On October 27, 1941, a German U-Boat launches a surprise attack on the U.S. Navy Destroyer Kearney, still the U.S. does not retaliate and declare war against Hitler's Germany. Again, on October 30, 1941, Germany launches an attack on U.S. Destroyer Reuben James, it sank as a result, leaving 100 American Navy men to perish. However, it would not be until 2 months later, when on December 7, 1941, the Japanese successfully infiltrate our shores and launch a "surprise" attack at Pearl Harbor, HI (our Pacific Navy fleet stronghold). The U.S. declares war on Japan December 8, 1941. (Smith, Carter, Smithsonian Presidents, pp 197)

Hitler himself is quoted paying homage to the foreign power creditor who was primarily responsible for sufficiently funding Germany's terrible designs for War! Hitler stated: "We have witnessed Catholocisms open support of every step taken by Nazi-Facism to impose authoritarian regimes upon all peoples."—Leo H. Lehman, Behind the Dictators, Agora Publishing, pp 36, 38, 39 (Hughes, Bill, The Secret Terrorists, pp 74) Why would the U.S. wait until the enemy came knocking at our doors until we would respond? Were we looking for a justification to utilize the A-Bomb as an act of war? Were the facist factions that controlled government in this country declaring war on the citizens of the U.S. who increasingly, on the horizon, were growing sharply against them ideals for world domination? Was there a fiscal conflict of interest since our support was largely being routed towards Germany through the misuse of unconstitutional fictional laws ratified by democratically elected dictators in Congress, and the Presidency as well as the Military, at its highest levels?

Since 1933, during the inception and height of the FDR Administration, power brokers in this country began to combine influence through the creation of "Round Table Groups", think tanks of industry sowing the seeds of secretive political influence. In 1934, for example, the

American Liberty League was created. Its primary financial support was vested in a few major players among the Wall Street elite, such as: the Rockefellers, Melons, Pews; as well as two former Democratic nominees for President, John W. Davis (an attorney for the J.P. Morgan banking interest) and Al Smith (Dupont business associate). This organization's goal and function were essentially to "combat radicalism, to teach the necessity of respect for the rights of persons and property, and generally to foster free enterprise." (Ventura, Jesse, American Conspiracies, pp 15) Unfortunately, the radicals these round table groups were combating were those who did not conform to their ideals, and/or were not part of their collective, elitist conspiracies. Meaning, the vast majority of the American Citizens then being fashioned into slavery, as well as factions of government and other secret groups who were competing for power and economic controls. Power and control over those aspects of world government and economies which are directly affected by currency and those who employ its vices are often policed by the threat of war. There are as many quiet wars, if not more, than there are official declarations throughout history. Those who police our economy, as well as the economies of other nations, are in the business of deposing detractors, and placing in power those who will do the will of the creditor. Kevin Phillips wrote an inciteful book about the Bush Family, "American Dynasty", which therein reveals that George Herbert Walker (Father-in-law to Prescott Bush) was part of "a frequently collaborative group of moneymen—Averell Harriman, Percy Rockefeller (National City Bank), others at Guarantee Trust— who had large international plans." National City Bank (1919) "joined in setting up the new W.A. Harriman and Company, soon to be under George Walker's presidency." Mr. Samuel Pryor (a Remington Man) combined his influence as "part of this cabal." In 1924, Averell Harriman and George Walker established the UBC, Union Banking Corporation, in New York "on behalf of the politically active German steel baron Fritz Țyssen", who coincidentally was a significant financial resource to Hitler's Nazi party. Seven years later, Prescott Bush and some of his elitist Skull and Bones fellowship out of Yale University "came together under one roof through the Brown Brothers Harriman merger in 1931." The author further remarked that "unfortunately, we have no reliable way of knowing exactly why, after 1933, men like Averell Harriman, George Walker, and Prescott Bush, the Dulles Brothers (side note: Allen Dulles, an attorney, would later become head of the CIA under Eisenhower and was a member of the Warren Commission which investigated the JFK assassination—cover up!—not to mention George Herbert Walker Bush, Sr. would become the head of the CIA and years later President of the United States; and son to Bush, Sr., George Walker Bush, Jr. would become Governor of Texas and thereafter, President of the United States as well—talk about keeping it in the firm/family!) James Forrestal, Henry Ford, and several Rockefellers maintained investment relationships with Hitler's Germany, in a few cases up to (and even after) Pearl Harbor." (Phillips, Kevin, American Dynasty, pp 19-20) Following the 1941 release of a New York Herald Tribune article which headlined, 'Hitler Angel has $3 Million in U.S. Bank', in 1942 the federal government "seized the assets of the Union Banking Corporation" exercising the power of the Trading With Țe Enemy Act of 1917. (Phillips, Kevin, American Dynasty, pp 20) In Proverbs 30: 13-14 we read: "Țere is a generation, Ț how lofty are their eyelids! And their eyelids are lifted up. There is a generation, whose teeth are as swords, and their jaw teeth as knives, to devour the poor from off the earth and the needy from among men." In the spirit of these words of wisdom and warning let us consider the testimony of generals who have been employed in the service of the creditors. So, we ask again, how does our government arrive at the idea, reasons or justifications leading up to a cause for war? The truth of the matter has largely been explained by one Major General Smedley Butler. To give you a little background about the Major General, he was the most highly decorated Marine in American History. In fact, "He has come under fire more than 120 times, received over 180 decorations, including 2 Medals of Honor." (American Conspiracies, Ventura, Jesse, pp 13) In a speech to the Legion Veterans the Major General Butler stated the following: "I spent 33 years being a high-class muscle man for Big Business, for Wall Street and the bankers. In short, I was a racketeer for capitalism.

I helped purify Nicaragua for the international banking house of Brown Brothers in 1909-1912. I helped make Mexico and especially Tampico safe for American oil interests in 1916. I helped make Haiti and Cuba a decent place for the National City Bank boys to collect revenue in. I helped rape half a dozen Central American Republics for the benefit of Wall Street. In China in 1927 I helped see to it that Standard Oil went its way unmolested. I had a swell racket . . . I might have give Al Capone a few hints. The best he could do was operate a racket in three cities. The Marines operated on three continents." (American Conspiracies, Ventura, Jesse, pp 14) Ironically, certain power brokers approached Major General Smedley Butler in order to sway him to overthrow the FDR Administration a la coup d' etat. However, his allegiances lay with FDR. Another prominent military leader, VFW Commander James Va n Zandt admitted he too was approached by "agents of Wall Street" regarding a likely FDR coup d' etat. Major General Butler brought a complaint about a potential government.

Overthrow threatening the presidency to the national media. Though, at first glance none of the national media outlets took him seriously.

The House Committee of the U.S. Congress conducted an investigation which revealed General Smedley Butler had in fact received an $18,000 bribe offer, as well as verified other key points to his allegations. Finally, around Thanksgiving in 1934 Time Magazine published an article with respect to the aforementioned plot against the presidency, but such only appeared in small print as a footnote stating that the House Committee was "convinced . . . that General Butler's story of a Facist march on Washington was alarmingly true." (American Conspiracies, Ventura, Jesse, pp 16) It is of great importance to note that the director of the FBI, J. Edgar Hoover, saw vast Nazi movements growing facist influence here in the U.S., following the election of Adolf Hitler as Chancellor of Germany in 1933. Then, in 1936 President Lazaro Cardenas of Mexico was enacting anti-clerical decrees, which caused great concern for the Catholic Church. Father E. Coughlin of Royal Oak, MI, "a fiery radio priest", was initially a supporter of FDR's "New Deal"; however, once President Roosevelt took a neutral stance with regards to President Cardenas' regime that all began to change . . . Now Father Coughlin became an adamant opponent to the "New Deal" and even approached one General Smedley Butler to lead an invasion into Mexico in order to depose President Cardenas, a la coup d' etat, so that the Catholic Church may be restored to its prior power and dominance. Rather than follow the Father's admonition and go through with the expedition Major General Butler instead reported the Father's intentions to J. Edgar Hoover. Hoover then sent a memo to FDR regarding the aforementioned report. However, no official action against Father Coughlin was ever taken by any level of government for his designs. Not to mention, FDR had already survived one assassination attempt which occurred, ironically, during his first campaign for the presidency. (Gentry, Curt, J. Edgar Hoover: The Man and the Secrets, pp 205-206) FDR relied heavily upon Hoover for intel regarding all Communist and/or Facist combinations here in the U.S. With respect to these investigations, Hoover stated: " What he (FDR) was interested in was obtaining a broad picture of the Communist and Facist movements and their activities as they might affect the economic and political activity of the country as a whole." (Gentry, Curt, J. Edgar Hoover: The Man and The Secrets, pp 207) According to author Douglas Rushkoff, in his book Life Inc., "By the time World War II was breaking out in Europe, American businessmen had a hard time deciding which side to support" (Germany, Italy, Japan: the Papacy or England, France, Russia: the Royal Crown Monarchy?) . . . Rushkoff went on to say that "American corporatists also saw in facism a counterbalance to FDR's strong-handed tactics and aggressive social welfare programs; Henry Ford and other corporate chiefs preferred the top-down "scientific management" of labor echoed by at least some of the facist policies of Benito Mussolini." (Rushkoff, Douglas, Life Inc., pp 109) Other corporatists support for the growing facist regime (both in Europe and the U.S.) grew out of, for example, Standard Oil of New Jersey (a Rockefeller Company). The author goes on to elaborate further:" SONJ . . . created a public-relations department to deflect mainstream media attention over the company's having supplied synthetic fuel to the Nazis (by way of I.G. Farben) even after the war had begun." (Rushkoff, Douglas, Life Inc., pp 109) On February 17, 1950, in a meeting before the United Nations and related organizations, Mr. James P. Warburg presented the following testimony for record: "We shall have world government, whether or not we like it.

The question is only whether world government will be achieved by consent or by conquest."

In sharp contrast, President Harry Truman declared: " We believe that all people who are prepared for self-government should be permitted to choose their own form of government by their own freely expressed choice, without inference from any foreign source." Unfortunately, that dream perished as soon as full control over the money was handed to a corporate agency of government, doing the bidding of the foreign powers' creditor, under Woodrow Wilson, hence, the Federal Reserve System. No President would challenge the foreign powers creditors (the Papacy, the Royal Crown of England, and other Monarchs and corporate elitist's secret combinations) until JFK was elected President.

VI

THE KENNEDY ERA

In 1961 President Dwight D. Eisenhower made the following statement in his farewell address: "In the councils of government, we must guard against the acquisition of unwarranted influence, whether sought or unsought, by the military-industrial complex. ☐e potential for disastrous rise of misplaced power exists and will persist. We must never let the weight of this combination endanger our liberties or democratic processes. We should take nothing for granted." (Ventura, Jesse, American Conspiracies, pp 22) There are several possibilities that have come to light which point to the reasons why President John F. Kennedy was shot and killed by a "lone gunman." Though, "there are two main reasons why Kennedy was assassinated. These reasons are involved with the Vietnam War and the Federal Reserve Bank." (The Secret Terrorists, Hughes, Bill, pp 85) President Kennedy ran on a platform
which was backed up with controversy. Whereas Kennedy declared he would not do the bidding of the Pope of the Vatican as President of the United States (since Kennedy was Catholic, this potential for bias was a real concern in the minds of many voters).

He kept his promise, even to his death. President John F. Kennedy was assassinated on Friday, November 22, 1963, at 12:30 pm. Colonel L. Fletcher Prouty explained that "on November 22, 1963, the government of the United States was taken over by the superpower group that wanted the escalation of the warfare in Indochina and a continuing military buildup." [Ibid. p 264] (The Secret Terrorists, Hughes, Bill, pp 85) Money was at the root of this evil! In fact, JFK issued Executive Order 11110, giving the U.S. Treasury back the authority to issue silver certificates which did not contain the Federal Reserve emblem included thereon. $4.3 million worth of silver certificates were released as currency in the U.S. at the time. Whereas, these notes were backed by silver, but the Federal Reserve notes were not backed by anything. The inevitability was that the Federal Reserve would eventually bankrupt as a result of JFK's executive order. However, the Fed did not go bankrupt, but five months following the executive order reinstituting the Gold Standard, JFK was assassinated. Ironically, the order in question is still in effect as law today, having never been repealed. Though, no president then or since has dared to utilize their powers to re-establish competition for currency issuance with the Fed. (Phillips, Kevin, American Dynasty, pp 168).

Shortly before JFK's death he began the de-escalation of the War in Vietnam. The day following JFK's demise the following took place: "at 8:30 am, Saturday, the 23rd of November 1963 the limousine carrying CIA director John McCone pulled into the White House grounds . . . He was . . . there to transact one piece of business prior to becoming involved in all the details entailed in a presidential transition—the signing of a National Security Memorandum 278, a classified document which immediately reversed John Kennedy's decision to de-escalate the war in Vietnam. The effect of Memorandum 278 would give the Central Intelligence Agency carte blanche to proceed with a full-scale war in the Far East . . . In effect, as of November 23, 1963, the Far East would replace Cuba as the thorn in America's side. It would also create a whole new source of narcotics for the Mafia's worldwide markets."—Robert Morrow, First Hand Knowledge, Shapolsky Publishers, pp 249 (The Secret Terrorists, Hughes, Bill, pp 89) The second reason for Kennedy's death is explained poignantly by one Colonel James Gritz, who stated: "When Kennedy called for a return of America's currency to the Gold Standard, and the dismantling of the Federal Reserve System—he actually, minted non-money debt that does not bear the mark of the Federal Reserve; when he dared to actually exercise the leadership authority granted to him by the U.S. Constitution . . . Kennedy prepared his own death warrant, it was time for him to go." (The Secret Terrorist, Hughes, Bill, pp 90) It is also important to note that JFK also wanted to dismantle the CIA (clandestine army of the creditor).

This would not be the last time someone in government would try to change American policy that affected business for the Federal Reserve, its agents and/ or expose it for its unconstitutionality and exploitative monopoly. In a controversial case, The First National Bank of Montgomery, Minnesota v. Jerome Daly (an attorney), by the court dated December 9, 1968, a ruling by Martin V. Mahoney, Justice of the Peace, Credit River Township, Scotts County, Minn., exposed the Federal Reserve in a way not before realized by the American public. As a result of the proceedings, in examination, it was admitted by the Bank of Montgomery President that "we can create money out of thin air." In other words, no fund, or gold, silver or any commodity or resource is in back of it or balanced against it in order to justify a bank's creation of money (in effect, Fed money is debt upon the backs of the people). This flys in the face of the U.S. Constitution,

Article I, Section 10, which states: "No State shall make anything but Gold and Silver Coin a Tender in Payment of Debts." (Redemption Manual, 4th Ed., pp 196) In this case aforementioned, it was also determined as part of the Judge's ruling regarding the bank's money, "No substantial fund of gold or silver is back of it, or any fund at all" . . . The Judge's ruling, "which is legally sound, has the effect of declaring all private mortgages on real and personal property, and all U.S. and State bonds held by the Federal Reserve, National and State Banks to be Null and Void . . ." Finally, it was boldly determined, thanks to Judge Martin V. Mahoney, in conjunction with his ruling, that both the "Federal Reserve Act of 1913 and the National Bank Act is in its operation and effect contrary to the whole letter and spirit of the Constitution of the United States." (Redemption Manual, 4th Ed., pp 189, 199).

Tragically, just 6 months following the afore ruling, Judge Martin V. Mahoney died in an apparent boating accident, though his body was discovered to be pumped full of poison. (Redemption Manual, 4th Ed., pp 191) What happened to the plaintiff, Jerome Daly, an attorney, plays out in a different case: United States v. Jerome Daly, 481 F. 2d. 28. In a cross examination of one Mr. Roland D. Graham, Vice-President and General Counsel of the Federal Reserve Bank of Minnesota, by the defendant representing himself, Jerome Daly, taken February 11, 1970, Mr. Graham testified: "The Federal Reserve System is the only instrumentality endowed by law with discretionary power to create the money that serves as bank reserves or as public pocket cash. Thus, the ultimate capability of expending or reducing the economy's supply of money rests with the Federal Reserve." As a result of these findings and the defendant, Jerome Daly's position, he was disbarred, never to practice law in the U.S. as an attorney ever again. With respect to Jerome Daly's allegiances, as a result of the above and the aforementioned "Credit River Township" case(s) in question, it became clear to the Minnesota's Board of Law Examiners that Jerome Daly could no longer serve the foreign power creditor(s) (i.e., the Minnesota BAR, the IBA, headquartered in London, England, and for that matter the Royal Crown of England, Exequer of the Vatican) as an Esquire (a Noble in society). At least they didn't kill him? In the case of Edwards v. Kearzev, 96 U.S. 595, it was found that "The Federal Reserve Notes (fiat money), which are attempted to be made legal tender, are exactly what the authors of the Constitution of the United States intended to prohibit . . . Congress is incompetent to authorize a State to make notes a legal tender." Also, make reference to 36 Am. Jur. on Money, Section 9. wherein it delineates: "Bank Notes are a good tender on money unless specifically objected to. Their consent and usage is based upon the convertibility of such notes to coin (gold and silver specie) at the pleasure of the holder upon presentation to the bank for redemption. When the inability of a bank to redeem its notes is openly avowed, they instantly lose their character as money and their circulation as currency ceases." (Redemption Manual, 4th Ed., pp 203-204) Finally, in 1971 the United States put a stop to redemption of U.S. currency in exchange for specie (gold and silver coin) at foreign central banks. This process of redemption was common practice overseas up until this time. (Phillips, Kevin, American Theocracy, pp 269).

Consider how our government has worked tirelessly since the time of the Civil War to divide our nation in order to maintain control over the collective States, all in an effort to diminish the Sovereign people of America. David Goldfield penned a book in 2002, "Still Fighting The Civil War: The American South and Southern History", and in it he made the following interpretation: "There is a war going on here. The Civil War is like a ghost that has not yet made its peace and roams the land seeking solace, retribution, and vindication. It continues to exist, an event without temporal boundaries, an interminable struggle that has generated perhaps as many casualties since its alleged end in 1865 as during the four preceding years when armies clashed on the battlefield. For the society that became the South after 1865—and truly, one could not speak of a distinct South before that time—the Civil War and the Reconstruction that followed shaped the form it takes today." (Phillips, Kevin, American Theocracy, pp 132) Is there evidence that Lincoln's Civil War policy still takes shape in U.S. Domestic Policy in the here and now, within our borders and among its citizens? In 1933, under President Franklin Delano Roosevelt, the U.S. Congress proposed the Bank Conservation Act, amending section 5, subsection B of the Trading With The Enemy Act of 1917 (originally passed under Lincoln) which accommodates Proclamation 2039. Wherein it states: "During time of War or during any other period of National Emergency declared by the President, the President may, through any agency he may designate . . . , investigate, regulate, or prohibit, under such rules and regulations as he may prescribe, by means of Licenses or otherwise, any transactions . . . , defined by the President . . . , by any person within the United States or any place subject to the jurisdiction thereof; and the President may require any person engaged in any transaction referred to, in this subdivision to furnish under oath, complete information relative thereto, including the production of any books of account, contracts, letters, or other papers, in connection therewith in custody or control of such person, either before or after such transaction is completed." (Redemption Manual, 4th Ed., pp 165).

Another example that demonstrates the Spirit of the Civil War is alive and well within the halls of Congress and the Presidency is further exemplified as follows: "The ownership of property is in the State; individual so-called ownership is only by virtue of government, i.e., law amounting to mere user; and use must be in accordance with law and subordinate to the necessities of the State." (March 9, 1933—Senate Document No. 43, 73rd Congress: 1rst Session) [Redemption Manual, 4th Ed., pp 295] Also, consider the following press release which covers the signing of the Coinage Act, July 23, 1965, by President Lyndon Johnson, former Vice-President to JFK, whereas President Johnson declared: "when I have signed this bill before me, we will have made the first fundamental change in our coinage in 173 years. The Coinage Act of 1965 supersedes the Act of 1792, and that Act had the title: An Act Establishing a Mint and Regulating the Coinage of the United States . . . Now I will sign this bill to make the first change in our coinage since the 18th Century. To those members of Congress, who are here on this historic occasion, I want to assure you that in making this change from the 18th Century we have no idea of returning to it." (Redemption Manual, 4th Ed., pp 222).

The Brothers Kennedy were both opposed to any such bill, as signed into law by President Johnson; both of them were assassinated. When President Johnson signed into law the abandonment of the Gold Standard roughly $11 billion in Gold was thereafter allocated for meeting "foreign obligations", thus temporarily postponing a financial crisis. The following quote from the book, "None Dare Call It Treason", elaborates: "Without the restraint imposed on the issuance of paper money by the gold reserve requirement, future national deficits could be financed with printing press dollars. Printing press inflation, as contrasted with the gradual long-term debasement of currency, could reduce the value of the dollar to 10 cents or even one cent within months. Such runaway inflation would destroy confidence in free enterprise and representative government. The insurance savings of millions of individuals, rich and poor, would be wiped out. The resulting 'national emergency' could be used as justification for abolishing the constitutional processes and establishing a totalitarian, socialistic government. The Americans who might be expected to oppose such a takeover would have no resources to finance opposition. Their savings would have been confiscated by runaway inflation" (such a scenario parallels Germany's condition, ca. 1920). (Stormer, John A., Death of A Nation, pp 16).

Finally, in direct correlation with the Executive Orders made by presidents, since the time of Lincoln and not unlike this one made by President Johnson, in 1973, Senate Report 93-549, 1rst Session of the 93rd Congress stated the following: "A majority of the people of the United States have lived all their lives under emergency rule . . . And, in the United States, actions taken by Government in times of great crisis have— from at least the Civil War— in important ways, shaped the present phenomenon of a permanent state of national emergency." (Redemption Manual, 4th Ed., pp 128) Upon considering the power of the Federal Reserve and its constituent agencies of oppression (with the foreign power creditor(s) at the helm), beyond that of our Congress and/or Commander-in-chief, let us consider the following revelation(s): with respect to HJR 192 and the Bank Holiday, both enacted by FDR through his power of Executive Order, President Hoover openly admits the Federal Reserve's role in government, upon stating, "whereas, in the opinion of the Board of

Directors of the Federal Reserve Bank of New York, the continued and increasing withdrawal of currency and gold from the banks of the country has now created a national emergency . . ." (Private Papers of President Herbert Hoover, March 3, 1933) (Redemption Manual, 4th Ed., pp 152) Therefore, we must ask: "What does the federal military construct have to offer the Federal Reserve in payment of its debt?

⟦Patton⟧ "The money will be worth 100 cents on the dollar because it is backed by the credit of the Nation. It will represent a mortgage on all homes and other property of all the people of the Nation." Therefore, as citizens of the UNITED STATES OF AMERICA, we are debtor slaves to our creditor masters, under contract with government to consecrate to the lenders, under penalty of (fictional, commercial) law and its agents who administer the weight of its letter, all that we purchase with money (backed by the labor of the people).

Taxation is representative of our actual "tenancy" upon land, and "lease-hold" of other property; and such can become property of the State and/or the creditor (banks under the central bank system) upon forfeiture through discontinuance of paying taxes and/or other fees for use of any property in the possession (care, custody, and control) of citizens, or for any reason as deemed necessary by the State, under law. Whereas we as citizens are property of the STATE, ourselves. The two most influential men behind the passage of the Federal Reserve Act of 1913 (legislation which opened the door to enslaving our nation) were Mr. Paul Warburg and Colonel Mr. Edward Mandel House. An excerpt from Mr. Warburg's intentions, to assure those serving on the Federal Reserve Board can do so unaffected by the authority of the President of the United States (the supreme democratic representative of the people), wherein he stated: "I am also suggesting that the Central Board be increased from four members to five, and their terms lengthened from eight to ten years. This would give stability and would take away the power of a President to change the personnel of the board during a single term of office." However, the Banking Act of 1935 lengthened board member terms to 14 years. [Roosevelt, Wilson and the Federal Reserve Law, Col. Elisha Ely Garrison, pp 137] (Redemption Manual, 4th Ed., pp 185-186) Samuel Adams once remarked that any people preferring the Un-American, Unconstitutional "tranquility of servitude" should make ready to "crouch down and lick the hands which feed you." In closing, he stated: "May your chains sit lightly upon you, and may posterity forget that you were our countrymen." (Beck, Glenn, Glenn Beck's Common Sense, pp 31).

VII

THE SECRET SERVICES

Albert Einstein is quoted as follows, "A foolish faith in authority is the worst enemy of truth." (Ventura, Jesse, American Conspiracies—Epilogue) Ponder the poignancy of these words as we move forward and consider the mission of those agencies of government which employ clandestine agents here in the U.S. Certain events of catastrophic proportion were orchestrated throughout history in order to justify (sell to the American populous) legislation for the perpetuation or creation of agencies of government; whose mission were to root out spies, frauds, and other offenders of the American social order. Let us look at the circumstances which led up to the terrible attack upon Pearl Harbor and the legislation for the expansion of clandestine agents on U.S. soil which was ratified soon thereafter. With respect to the intel gathered previous to the Japanese attack on "Pearl Harbor", by December 4, 1941, the U.S. Special National Intelligence Estimate had compiled the following: "For the past two weeks, Japan has been warning its diplomats that war may be imminent. Interception of Japanese diplomatic traffic indicates the message "East Wind Rain" has been repeated on a regular basis. Intelligence officials believe this code means Japan has made a decision to go to war in the near future. In addition, there have been these other signs that Japan may be preparing to go to war:

1. On November 22, Foreign Minister Togo informed Ambassador Nomura that negotiations between Japan and the United States must be settled by November 29 because after that "things are going to automatically happen."
2. For the past two weeks, the Japanese have been padding their radio messages with garbled or old messages to make decoding more difficult.
3. Three days ago, the Japanese Imperial Navy changed its ship call signs. This is an unprecedented change, since they had just been changed. Normally, they are switched every six months.
4. Two days ago, the Japanese Foreign Ministry ordered its consulate in six cities—including Washington—to destroy all but the most important codes, ciphers, and classified material.
5. Three days ago, the U.S. became unable to locate previously tracked Japanese submarines.
6. Scattered, unconfirmed reports indicate naval air units in southern Japan have been practicing simulated torpedo attacks against ships there.

These warning signs justify immediate, extraordinary steps, including placing the Pacific command on immediate alert."

However, FDR did not take steps to assure our Pacific fleet was put on alert, nor otherwise warned of the dangers, despite intelligence report strong recommendations. He simply did nothing, he, and the military, in the face of these estimates stood down. Perhaps, such an event would justify the use of nuclear strikes against our newfound, bold adversary? Maybe Japan was supposed to push further inland, into California, instead of just decimating the Pacific Naval Fleet, Pearl Harbor, Hawaii? This attack was, however, substantial justification for creation of the CIA in 1947. The founder of this Central Intelligence Agency idea was primarily "cooked up" by one Colonel William J. ("Wild Bill") Donovan (then, a New York lawyer and politician). Donovan served in the military during WWI and was highly decorated, after commanding an entire battalion, with the Congressional Medal of Honor. (Kessler, Ronald, Inside the CIA, pp 97-99) The plan for the CIA was modeled after the OSS (Office of Strategic Services) and was initially presented to FDR in 1941. FDR took the first step towards the CIA's creation by creating a "Coordinator of Information" role as "part of the office of the President."

Donovan, during WWII, headed the OSS. However, it would not be until after FDR's fourth election as President of the United States, and shortly thereafter, untimely death (at age 55) that President Truman would take over the reigns and under whom, in 1946 the Central Intelligence Group would be created and written into law. The CIG would be renamed, though, as the CIA, under the National Security Act of 1947. Ironically, the same year Japan attacks the U.S., in 1941, Joseph Stalin, supreme leader of the Soviet Union, ignored intelligence reports regarding Hitler's Nazi-German Blitzkrieg invasion plans.

This blind-eyed inaction resulted in the loss of tens of thousands of Russian lives unnecessarily, as a direct result of Stalin's omission(s). (Kessler, Ronald, Inside the CIA, pp 101) The question there for both FDR and Stalin remains: were they cooperating with invasions in the same year by this combination of facist enemies to both the U.S. and Soviet Union? FDR and Stalin's own pre-knowledge of likely attacks, and apparent lack of preparations against any such action and/or pre-emptive strikes taken, certainly beg the above question! Edward W. Proctor (a former CIA Director for Intelligence) once elaborated regarding intelligence estimates: "the most important thing was not whether we were right or wrong about the occurrence of events, but to help the people making policy decisions by giving them background information. Sometimes you give them information that is right, and they make the wrong decisions. Sometimes you give them information that is wrong, and they make the right decisions for different reasons . . . the whole purpose is to help these people make better decisions." (Kessler, Ronald, Inside The CIA, pp 101).

So, this helps us perhaps see with different eyes what the leaders of our countries are up against upon trying to disseminate through the trees to see the forest, the bigger picture that intelligence estimates paint. Russell J. Brown, a retired CIA analyst and consultant made the following observation about CIA tactics (from the 40's, 50's, and into the 60's): "There is a certain momentum that carried from WWII and OSS type thinking into the early sixties. The idea was you had a job to do, and you go out and do the job, and you clean up the problems later . . ." (Kessler, Ronald, Inside The CIA, pp 102-103) Getting the U.S. into "problems" seemed to be the CIA's mission, and certainly their forte' ever since the organization's inception.

For example, Mr. Frank Church, a former U.S. Senator, and staunch critic of the CIA, in 1975 candidly revealed: "In the last twenty-five years, no important new Soviet weapons system, from their H-Bomb to their most recent missiles, has appeared which had not been heralded in advance by NIE's [National Intelligence Estimates]. (Kessler, Ronald, Inside The CIA, pp 106) Yet, the U.S. Government did little to curtail the Soviet Union's proliferation of WMD's. Another example of the CI A's mission, with respect to spying on U.S. citizens, is exemplified upon considering that The Rockefeller Commission was organized to investigate into the CI A's "Operation Chaos", which was perpetrated upon Americans. Jerry G. Brown, who joined the Office of Security in 1956, reported that the premise behind Operation Chaos was to investigate "domestic dissidents" or in other words "unsophisticated detractors". Such was claimed by Mr. Brown to be "a purposeful attempt by the agency and the Nixon Administration to subvert the domestic political process by spying on American citizens." This operation, in and of itself, was against the CI A's own charter. Mr. Brown went on to boldly declare: "Those who would destroy us and our efforts were not the Soviets and our other worldwide enemies, but our own elected legislative representatives." (Kessler, Ronald, Inside The CIA, pp 151-152)

  FDR and Stalin certainly rang that solemn bell as true, since they, their homegrown armies, and constituent faithful, legislative followers became, it would seem, enemies to the populous in both nations; and whose mutual spirit of totalitarianism, for a time, dominated the political, social, and economic landscapes to the extent they were wholeheartedly at odds with the idea of freedom and its divinely inspired tenets. Since this time, the world began to spiral out of control and played into the hands of the creditors by becoming debtor nations, either by choice or by conquest thenceforth unto this very day. This is not a new concept, however, but a series of trials at trying to perfect the process of recreating history, until it is 33 A.D. once again and we all render that which we have to Cesar!

An important point we should add to our attentions is found in the answer to this question: how do the lawyers come into play within the decision-making process of CIA operations? Russell J. Bruemmer (special assistant to the FBI) explained as follows: "What we set out to do was get the lawyers involved in the decision-making process early. Not to make the decisions, but to point out the legal pitfalls and help structure proposals to address them. Over and over again we told my office . . . that the job of a lawyer is not to say no, but to say yes if or no but and help people do what they want to do within the structure of the law." (Kessler, Ronald, Inside The CIA, pp 229) In other words, with the understanding of the lawyer's ability to construe and construct the law to conform to the mission of the clandestine agents of the CIA, FBI and other agencies of government operating in the U.S. with similar mandates and immunities; "they" become immune to indictment, prosecution, charges, and conviction for criminal, impeachable behavior, inasmuch as they follow their "lawful" mandate.

One example of the CIA's ability to operate on the fringe, immune to prosecution, is when one considers the Vietnam War. The influence of the Vatican's policies in the Vietnam War led to a barrage of covert military actions against the Buddhist entrenched regimes, in hopes of spreading its clerical dominance among the Vietnamese people. A Washington Post article, dated September 10, 1963, reported the Coup d'etat attempt: "The United States has been understandably embarrassed by the disclosure that the CIA has been secretly aiding the South Vietnam Special Forces that conducted the raids on Buddhist pagodas . . . when the CIA invests its prestige in supporting a given course, there is an all-too-human tendency to seek vindication for a commitment of money and judgment. This seems to lie behind the present muddle over CIA misadventures in Saigon. The agency's mission chief in that country had established close and cordial relations with Ngo Dinh Nhu, President Diem's brother and sponsor of the Special Forces. Some $3 million a year was earmarked for helping the Special Forces. But reportedly the CIA had no advance warning that the forces would invade the pagodas and the initial intelligence reaction was confused—contributing to the confusion in Washington over what transpired that fateful day. Nevertheless, the payments evidently continued in the face of government policy to the contrary, and the Administration has been reduced to a stutter in trying to explain what has happened. Ironically, notwithstanding the CIA subsidy, the pro-Diem press in Saigon has been bitterly attacking the American agency for allegedly taking part in an attempted coup against the regime." (Blackstock, Paul W., The Strategy of Subversion, pp 204-205) In this case, the media was used to confuse Americans, rather than convey the truth.

In March of 1963 one Nikita S. Krushchev, the former Soviet Union Premier, boldly declared at a conference with party leaders, acclaimed artists, and writers: "We live in a period of struggle for the minds of men, for their re-education (something we in the U.S. call "brainwashing"). This is a complicated process, far more difficult than retooling plants and factories . . . you must understand that a fierce struggle is going on in the world between two incompatible ideologies—the socialist (communist) and the bourgeois (facist) ideologies." (Blackstock, Paul W., The Strategy of

Subversion, pp 29) the use of the media by writers (books, articles), artists (movies, plays, performances) and party leaders (advertisements, commercials, documentaries, conferences) all combined to work upon the minds of men, to program it, to change it, so, men and women and children see the world through the blinders of confusion and misguided emotion. Thus, to produce afore predicted effect thereupon which serves to the puppet-master's liking. Political Warfare Theory or "Manipulative Persuasion" addresses the challenges between political and social aims of a particular country which may be exploited to "soften the fabric of society, undermining their morale and resistance to further intervention by the aggressor." In fact, it can be further stated that "psychological warfare depends upon intelligence for all aspects of its operation." Psychological warfare targets "people's hopes, aspirations, and political, sociological and cultural backgrounds." Psychological Warfare may be defined as "that body of knowledge resulting from the collection, evaluation, collation, and interpretation of ties and patterns of rational and non-rational behavior that may characterize a group that one hopes to influence through propaganda appeals and other non-lethal devices." (Blackstock, Paul W., The Strategy of Subversion, pp 121-122).

Adolf Hitler used psychological warfare to "sell" war to the German populous. On August 22, 1939, the Chancellor of Germany stated: "I shall give a propagandistic cause for starting the war whether it will be plausible or not. The victor shall not be asked later on whether he told the truth or not. In starting or making war, not right is what matters, but victory." (Blackstock, Paul W., The Strategy of Subversion, pp 208) With respect to the German-Polish crisis, Von Weizsaeker, of the Foreign Office, made the following observation regarding Hitler's tactics: "Those who have written history of this last phase has so far understandably confined themselves to the diplomatic course of events, to the official books of various colors, to the confiscated documents, memoirs, etc. But in doing so they have underestimated certain political realities—namely, how, as a result of Hitler's frivolous game, in the last ten days of August 1939, so much unrest had been engendered in the German minority, so many frontier infringements had occurred, so many people had been carried away into Central Poland, and so many other incidents had been reported that all these things weighed heavier in the scales than the reverberating dispute of the so-called statesman about how the original problem was to be solved. One may well ask whether the chariot had not already been rolling inexorably toward the abyss in the spring of 1939; but in the last week of August, it certainly was. Hitler was now the prisoner of his own methods. He could no longer pull the horse to one side without being thrown out of the chariot. And riding on the lead horse was the devil." (Blackstock, Paul, W, The Strategy of Subversion, pp 216).

Now, with respect to the CIA and its operations influencing the policies of government in the U.S., let us consider the words of former President Harry S. Truman, stated in December of 1963: "For some time I have been disturbed by the way the CIA has been diverted from its original assignment. It has become an operational arm and at times a policy-making arm of the Government. This has led to trouble and may have compounded our difficulties in several explosive areas. I never had any thought that when I set up the CIA that it would be injected into peacetime cloak and dagger operations. Some of the complications and embarrassment that I think we have experienced are in part attributable to the fact that this quiet intelligence arm of the President has been so removed from its intended role that it is interpreted as a symbol of sinister and mysterious foreign intrigue . . . I, therefore, would like to see the CIA be restored to its original assignment as the intelligence arm of the President . . . and that its operational duties be terminated or properly used elsewhere. There is something about the way the CIA has been functioning that is casting a shadow over our historic position, and I feel we need to correct it." (Blackstock, Paul W., The Strategy of Subversion, pp 278).

President Truman's position on the CIA (created under his watch) was further emphasized in an article published in the Saturday Evening Post, January 4-11, 1964, quoting Senator Eugene J. McCarthy, speaking from the Senate floor in March of 1963: "Wrapped in its cloak of secrecy, the U.S. Central Intelligence Agency modestly hints it has overthrown foreign governments, admits that it violates international law . . . The CIA, in short, is making foreign policy, and, in so doing, is assuming the role of the President and the Congress. It has taken on the character of an invisible government answering only to itself. This must stop. The CIA must be made accountable for its activities, not only to the President, but also to Congress through a responsible committee." (Blackstock, Paul W., The Strategy of Subversion, pp 278-279).

Anthony Blunt served as a Soviet agent and upon explaining his reasoning ideologically for doing so he conveyed the following: "In the mid-1930's it seemed to me . . . that the Communist Party and Russia constituted the only firm bulwark against Facism since the Western democracies (including the U.S.) were taking an uncertain and compromising attitude towards Germany. I was persuaded . . . that I could best serve the cause of anti-fascism by [working] for the Russians." (Richelson, Jeffrey T., A

Century of Spies, pp 91) Hence, as Krushchev stated, there are two opposing forces at work among the leaders of nations, the "socialist" (communist) and the "bougeois" (facist). There really is no middle ground, no significant third party, and no grey area. Though, the creditor(s) don't really care what side of the road you are standing on as long as they control the interstate traffic by the creation and perpetuation of money through a central banking system; and its constituent agents of "chaos" and "mahan" are at work to "collect", one way or another.

VIII
A WAR ON GUNS

One of the propagandistic themes being perpetuated by the media and the current regime of government holding the reigns against the backs of the American populous is the "war on guns". This is a battle against the production, sales, and ownership of guns by "free citizens in good standing" by those agents of government who do the bidding of the foreign powers creditor(s). The U.S. government utilizes incidents of violence involving firearms, in conjunction with the media (bias) to "sell the idea" to the American people, like a religion being sold door to door, one IP Address, one cable connection, one satellite wave receiver at a time. In particular, they combine to launch virulent attacks on the NRA (National Rifleman's Association) which occurs each time a "lone shooter" walks into a school, a university, a public establishment and senselessly takes innocent lives. As if it were the fault of the gun-makers, and legislators, even the Founders of this Country, for guns being proliferated among American citizens?

The real problem lies with those who do the bidding of the foreign powers creditor who write laws to prevent gun ownership among citizenry, in order to promote their own control and dominance among those who are inherently "the ultimate authority", despite those contracts with the U.S. Government which say otherwise. One example of how the media and government combine to oppress the American populous with gun-control measures is demonstrated in an article addressing the Mexican Mafia Cartels (Zeta and Sinaloa) struggle to traffic drugs and the innocent civilians who are caught in the crossfire. The article in question was written in "The Week" magazine publication, April 20, 2012, titled: "How They See Us: Exporting Death to Mexico". It states, "the Mexican President Felipe Calderon vehemently fires back at the NRA, laying blame at the doorstep of an American Political Lobbyist group for the 50,000 + civilians who have perished during the aforementioned conflict to date. President Calderon met with President Barack Obama and Canadian Prime Minister Stephen Harper to discuss the problem of U.S. made assault weapons being used to bathe Mexico in blood! He warned that our government should put a ban on all assault weapons, or the violence is likely to spill over into the U.S. President Calderon is quoted as stating in this meeting: "The very future of American Society will be threatened." It was further intonated that the NRA shares "an enormous responsibility for the violence that is taking place in Mexico." (Rivera, Angel Miguel, La Jornada, The Week Magazine, pp 16)

The U.S. Government's goal is to thwart every aspect of the U.S. Constitution for the American people, especially the 2nd Amendment. Whereas, to take away the power of the populous at large to protect themselves against foreign invaders (Local, State, Federal and especially the United Nations), which gives them (agents of the foreign power creditors) certain leverage to control future inevitabilities. Inasmuch as we realize our current system is a shadow government regime doing the bidding of the Royal Crown of England and the Papacy of the Vatican, as well as other creditors, like China, then we can see how precarious our situation and status as U.S. citizens have become. Let me give you an example. On October 6, 1966, the Pittsburg Catholic, an official publication of the Pittsburg, PA diocese contained a quote from one Msgr. Charles Owens Rice as saying: "It may be strange coming from a Catholic Priest, but I am convinced we should pray for the survival of the present government in China . . . The present government, even though Communist, has brought order to its vast nation, order and admirable measures of internal justice and peace. Mao Tse-Tung and his followers have changed China utterly, and the change has been for the better . . . To be sure he has established and maintained tight control and has insisted on an austere program. He incessantly propagandizes. He, alas, uses hate as a weapon for control and motivation. Many are the mistakes of Mao and his coterie, but the evidence is that the men now ruling from Peking desire the welfare of the people of China." With respect to the "sacrifices of the Chinese people" by Mao Tse-Tung, Rice is further quoted as follows: "we should look on this with a certain sympathy and tolerance." The sacrifices of the Chinese people by Mao and his coterie amounted to the mass murder of 40 million innocent civilians.

The Catholic Church was not alone in their singular view. Consider Dr. John C. Bennett, one of the most influential leaders in the National and World Council of Churches during the 1960's, regarding the U.S.'s position on China, he stated: "The American stance of moralistic hostility that seeks to keep China isolated from the international community is the worst possible approach to the problems which China raises. We should rather regard the Chinese revolution and all that has followed (the slaughter of 40-million human beings—Author) as a momentous human earthquake rather than as behavior to be judged by our usual moral yardsticks. It calls for awe initially, rather than condemnation." Dr. Bennett goes on to say, "Communism has proved to be the instrument by which this notion has been united (by killing the opposition)." (Stormer, John A., Death of A Nation, pp 92-94. Why is it that the Chinese government under Mao Tse-Tu ng could do no wrong? Was it because he was doing the bidding of the credit master, the Papacy? Would ethnic cleansing eventually open the doors in China to greater Catholic influence and then control? Who can surmise the bigger picture, and the cost . . . who can count it? The only "thing" involved in such a holocaustic series of atrocities can only amount to eventual signs, dollar signs that is, for the government and the creditor that controls its movements. So, give up guns, you say . . . for the greater good of whom? What will be the promised blessing bestowed for being so obedient as to collectively surrender to the creditor(s)? Could it amount to the 20th Century mass murder of the Jews during WWII, or interment of the Japanese (American citizens) during WWII in our own country? Could our situation become like that of the "Trail of Tears" the Indians trod and/or the "Pioneer Trail" of the Mormons; both of the 19th Century whose homes, lands, possessions and in many cases their virtue and very lives were taken, under the orders and so-called protections of democratically elected state officials and military, "looking out for the public good". Whereas they were shuffled from State to State, in search of a home . . . on horseback, and on bare feet, leaving blood-stained footprints in the snow behind them? I ask, I beg the question . . . What good can government do when it is in the hands of a secret combination of demons whose goal is control, whose love is to be feared, and whose desire is for power and wealth, even all of it!? Does history repeat itself?

A Georgetown University professor and author, Caroll Quigley, wrote the book, "Tragedy and Hope", which sheds certain light upon Round Table Groups and Rhodes Scholarships, in particular, including their broad purposes and how American everyday life has been thereby affected. The author states that Cecil Rhodes worked with financiers such as the Rothchilds to monopolize the South African gold and diamond trade, for example. An interesting sidenote, Carrol Quigley was professor to one William (Bill) Clinton, former President of the U.S., and Rhode Scholar. In Tragedy and Hope, the author Caroll Quigley is quoted regarding these international financiers: "There does exist, and has existed for a generation, an international Anglophile network which operates, to some extent, in the way the radical Right believes the Communists act. In fact, this network, which may be identified as Round Table Groups, has no aversion to cooperating with the Communists, or any other groups, and frequently does so.

I know of the operations of this network because I have studied it for twenty years and was permitted for two years, in the early 1960's, to examine its papers and secret records. I have no aversion to it or to most of its aims and have, for much of my life, been close to it and much of its instruments . . . in general my chief difference of opinion is that it wishes to remain unknown, and I believe its role in history is significant enough to be known." (Quigley, Carrol, Tragedy and Hope, pp 16-17) In 1928, Quigley additionally reveals, the CFR or Council on Foreign Relations, was one of the front organizations established in an effort to expand the

First World War. The CFR's funding derived from groups "associated with J.P. Morgan and Company in association with the very small American Round Table Group."

In 1928, according to Quigley, the CFR's president was Al Smith, business associate to the Duponts (established the American Liberty League, with J.P. Morgan and Company). This is the same organization which approached Major General Smedley Butler and VFW Commander James Van Zandt, in hopes of carrying out a coup d'etat against the FDR leadership. The ultimate goal of this cartel managerie of money kings, according to Quigley was "nothing less than to create a world system of financial control in private hands able to dominate the political system of each country and the economy of the world as a whole. This system was to be controlled in a feudalist fashion by the central banks of the world acting in concert (IMF and FSB) by secret agreements arrived at in frequent private meetings and conferences. Each central bank . . . sought to dominate its government by its ability to control treasury loans, to manipulate foreign exchanges, to influence the levels of economic activity in the country and to influence cooperative politicians by subsequent economic rewards in the business world." (Quigley, Carroll, Tragedy and Hope, pp 17-18) Also, consider that the Bank for International Settlements, based in Basel, Switzerland, (BIS) was created to govern "a world system of financial control in private hands able to dominate the political system of each country and the economy of the world as a whole." Within the BIS a Financial Stability Board (FSB) was created in order "to promote global financial stability." (Quigley, Carroll, Tragedy and Hope, pp 180) ⌃ IMF are the administrative arm (agents) of the FSB, under the umbrella of the BIS.

This system of global central banks is set up to, essentially, direct and control all of the governments in the world caught in their web. Their first order of business for the past several generations, even before the creation of these United States of America, has been simply to take away the Sovereignty of the people and their ability to protect themselves against foreign agents of government (army of the foreign power creditors). Hence, the reason(s) why there is such a push for guns to be taken away from the people by our democratically elected officials, so many measures taken to sell this religion of disarmament in the media—because it is the will of the creditor(s).

In the August 2011 edition of the 'Woods n Water' magazine publication an article containing the NRA's candid response to a preliminary conference held by the United Nations, involving negotiations with the U.S. Government for an "Arms Trade Treaty". In other words, a conference to discuss how the U.S. should surrender policing its people to the UN and its agents, beginning with the discontinuance of fire arms sales, possession, and proliferation within our "free" borders. The article in question headlines as: "NRA vows to oppose proposed U.N. Arms Trade Treaty".

The treaty (ATT) in question would infringe upon the 2nd Amendment of the Constitution of the United States, giving way to precedent holding that "international law" supercedes, even replaces the highest law in America and the Sovereignty of its Citizenry! The NRA's Executive Vice-President, Wayne LaPierre wrote a letter addressing these issues affecting our right to carry, and more. La Pierre reminds the U.N. Chair that the "NRA was founded in 1871" defending the rights of "Freedom-loving" gun owners ever since (2011 registration record totaled roughly" 80 million").

La Pierre continues in his letter to the U.N. Chair, "In 1996, the NRA was recognized as an NGO of the United Nations . . ." and that the "NRA is the largest and most active firearms rights organization in the world . . ." He goes on to highlight a crucial list of stated objections to these U.N. proposals: "We reject the notion that American gun owners must accept any lesser amount of freedom in order to be accepted among the international community. Our Founding Fathers long ago rejected that notion and forged our great nation on the principle of freedom for the individual citizen—not for the government. Mr. Chairman, those working on this treaty have asked us to trust them . . . but they've proven unworthy of that trust. We are told, "trust us, ATT will not ban possession of any civilian firearms. Yet, the proposal and statements presented to date have argued exactly the opposite, and—perhaps most importantly— proposals to ban civilian firearms ownership have not been rejected. We are told "Trust us; an ATT will not interfere with state domestic regulation of firearms." Yet, there are constant calls for exactly such measures.

We are told "Trust us; an ATT will not require registration of civilian firearms." Yet, there are numerous calls for record-keeping and firearms tracking from production to eventual destruction. That's nothing more than gun registration by a different name. We are told "Trust us; an ATT will not create a new international bureaucracy." Well, that's exactly what is now being proposed with a tongue-in-cheek assurance that it will just be a SMALL bureaucracy. We are told "Trust us; an ATT will not interfere with a hunter or sport shooter traveling internationally with firearms." However, he would have to get a so-called "transit permit" merely to change airports from a connecting flight . . . It is regrettable proposals affecting civilian firearm ownership are woven throughout the proposed

ATT . . . It is also regrettable to find such intense focus on record-keeping, oversight, inspections, supervision, tracking, tracing, surveillance, marking, documentation, verification, paper trails, and data banks, new global agencies, and data centers.

Nowhere do we find a thought about respecting anyone's right to self-defense, privacy, property, due process, or observing personal freedoms of any kind. Mr. Chairman, I'd be remiss if I didn't also discuss the politics of the AT T. For the United States to be party to an AT T, it must be ratified by a two-thirds vote of the U.S. Senate. Some do not realize that under the U.S. Constitution, the ultimate treaty power is not the President's power to negotiate and sign treaties; it is the Senate's power to approve them . . . ⌷ Cornerstone of our freedom is the Second Amendment. Neither the United States, nor any other foreign influence, has the authority to meddle with the freedoms guaranteed by our Bill of Rights, endowed by our creator, and due to all humankind."—Still believe the international community in combination with the current government regime has our "best interests" at heart?

IX

CONSIDER THE CONSTITUTION

Amos Singletary, at the Massachusetts Convention for ratification of the Constitution For the United States of America, is quoted addressing the President, specifically, as follows: "these lawyers, and men of learning, and moneyed men, that talk so smoothly, to make us poor illiterate people swallow down the pill, expect to get into Congress themselves; they expect to be the managers of the Constitution and get all the power and all the money into their own hands, and then they will swallow up all us little folks, like the great Leviathon, Mr. President; yes, just as the whale swallowed up Jonah." With regards to the Constitution's ratification, Alexander Hamilton boldly remarked: "Among the most formidable of the obstacles which the new Constitution will have to encounter may readily be distinguished the obvious interest of a certain class of men in every State to resist all changes which may hazard a diminuition of the power, enmolument, and consequence of the offices they hold under the State establishments." (McGuire, Robert A., To Form A More Perfect Union, pp 172, 179) In other words, men addicted to power and money and the tenacious continuity of such positions in government were combining efforts to mold and shape aspects of the Constitution to benefit themselves and the creditor(s) they served since the inception of these United States, even unto this very day. Also at the Massachusetts Convention, Mr. Charles Turner, made the following observation upon considering our nation's necessity to bolster a national currency supported by standardized Specie, which is the function of Constitutional Law: ". . . I consider the deplorable state of our navigation and commerce . . . the tendency of depreciating paper, and tender acts, to destroy mutual confidence, faith and credit." (McGuire, Robert A., To Form A More Perfect Union, pp 186)

James Madison, at the Virginia Convention to ratify the U.S. Constitution, argued that "we must make effectual provision for the payment of the interest of our public debts." However, George Mason made it known that he believed we should avoid debt, but rather "we must pay it shilling for shilling . . . The nominal value must . . . be paid." James Madison responded to Mason's proposal with the following: "Do gentlemen wish the public creditors should be put in a worse situation. . . ? There cannot be a majority of the people of America that wish to defraud their public creditors." Continuing with the debate, Patrick Henry added his spice to the gumbo, being less than satisfied with Madison's retort, responded by revealing he has "heard there were vast quantities of that money packed up in barrels: those formidable millions are deposited in the Northern States" . . . whereas, they "acquired it for a most inconsiderable trifle." During the campaign in New York, this debate over public security holdings was reported in the New York Press, stating: "It [the Constitution] is in the interest of all Public Creditors, because they will see the credit of the States rise, and their Securities appreciate." (McGuire, Robert A., To Form A More Perfect Union, pp 146).

The creditor(s) have known, always known that to enslave our States with public credit, which amounts to un-payable debt upon the backs of the people, is to control law-makers, legislators, law-administrators and every government official dually elected or appointed to represent the interests of the nation (the people); whereas, payment of the interest primarily, instead of "shilling for shilling" as we did under Andrew Jackson, will perpetuate debt until every right under the Constitution, every aspect of popular sovereignty will be lost forever. Are we there yet? Alexander Hamilton rallied for ratification of the Constitution and explained its necessity for governance in this way: "The new constitution has in favour of its successes these circumstances—a very great weight of influence of the persons who framed it . . . the goodwill of the commercial interests throughout the states which will give all its efforts to the establishment of a government capable of regulating, protecting and extending commerce of the Union—the goodwill of most men of property in the several states who wish a government of the Union able to protect them against domestic violence and the depredations which the democratic spirit is apt to make on property . . . the hopes of the Creditors of the United States that a general government possessing the means of doing it will pay the debt of the Union." In direct opposition to Hamilton's position a few very important delegates and state office holders argued: "add to these causes the disclination of the people to taxes and of course to a strong government—the opposition of all men much in debt who will not wish to see a government established one object of which is to restrain this means of cheating Creditors." (McGuire, Robert A., To Form A More Perfect Union, pp 149-150).

Hamilton well understood that to default on loans to the foreign powers creditor(s) is to invite war, in all of its potential facets and strategems (remember the Revolutionary War and the War of 1812, for example). Charles A. Beard, in 1913 canonized several scholarly views regarding the U.S. Constitution and he maintained that the "primary beneficiaries under the Constitution would have been individuals with Commercial and financial interests—particularly those with public securities holdings." According to Beard, these holders of such interests had a clause included in the Constitution requiring the assumption of existing federal debt by the new national government. Though, a contrasting view is argued by one Mr. Forrest McDonald, who in 1958 conducted an empirical study of the founding of the Constitution, but in part came to similar conclusions with respect to certain common motivations involved with its constructing, whereas he stated that the people are the "ultimate source of authority embodied . . . in the Constitution . . ." McDonald further stated the Constitution's founding "was primarily a financial one. It was the desire of the security holders." (McGuire, Robert A., To Form A More Perfect Union, pp 25, 27) Finally, we take into account the fact that "our nation's citizens did not have the opportunity to directly choose the content of the Constitution or to directly vote on ratifying the Constitution; their representatives, our Founding Fathers, made these choices for them." (McGuire, Robert A., To Form A More Perfect Union, pp 35) Changes made to the Constitution which presented the greatest challenges, in particular, "were those changes that strengthened the framework for protection of private property and enforcement of contracts." Also, the passing of ex-post facto laws as well as prohibitory laws preventing States from enacting "law impairing the obligation of contracts." (McGuire, Robert A., To Form A More Perfect

Union, pp 42)

It is important to pause and take note that among the Framers there were "22 lawyers, 14 politicians, 13 planters, 9 merchants, 4 judges, 3 physicians, 2 less commercial farmers, and one retired printer at the Philadelphia Convention", for example. These men represented a vast array of interests and considerations from all walks of life throughout the landscape of the U.S. at the time. Though, "less than 30 Framers were ever involved in the deliberations". (McGuire, Robert A., To Form A More Perfect Union, pp 51-52) George Mason (Virginia) was opposed to Amendments to the Constitution and in fact, the sixteenth vote at Philadelphia was in favor of preventing any such Amendments thereto. George Mason related that he "thought the plan of amending the Constitution exceptionable and dangerous. Wherefore, it was his belief that amendments at the Federal level could infringe upon the rights of the several States, especially the minority States of the Union." He was more than prophetic in his view upon raising concerns that amendments would result in "Executive, Congressional and Judicial" infringements upon State's governments. He was right in making such bold assertions; however, James Madison supported the concept of "absolute national veto", which would prevent States from infringing upon each other. Madison stated his position "could not but regard an indefinite power to negative legislative acts of the States as absolutely necessary to [form] a perfect system." Madison's belief was that States would "otherwise infringe the rights and interests of each other . . ." (McGuire, Robert A., To Form A More Perfect Union, pp 70).

Not long after the ratification of the Constitution in several states, in order to "form A more perfect union", Thomas Jefferson warned Americans about the powerful ills associated with the operation of a central banking system in the U.S. In 1815 he stated: "The dominion which the banking institutions have obtained over the minds of our citizens . . . must be broken, or it will break us." (Stormer, John A., The Death of A Nation, pp 180) In this selfsame spirit of reason, the Church of Jesus Christ of Latter-Day Saints today, by way of example, does not go into debt, but relies upon the tithes and offerings of its people, its members (worldwide) and is in fact a creditor unto itself, it is self-insured and a self-assured global entity, an agent unto itself and truly is largely free from its oppressors, despite any and all misguided detractors.

X

THE BANKS AND THEIR AGENTS

On January 2 7, 1980 in Sydney, Australia two police officers come upon a Mercedes, parked, around 4 A.M. on a quietly traveled road with its parking lights on. Therein they found a man lay dead in a pool of his own blood. The deceased was identified as Francis J. Nugan (co-founder of the Nugan Hand Bank). In his pockets the police found the business card of William Colby, former director of U.S. Intelligence. On the rear of the business card was an intinerary for a trip to Asia planned by Colby to take place the following month. On the seat of the Mercedes was a Bible. Inside the Bible was found a meat-pie wrapper with the names of Colby and U.S. Representative Bob Wilson of California (Ranking Republican on the House Armed Services Committee).

The following directors of the Nugan Hand Bank (within 24 hours of this gruesome discovery) were contacted: Leroy J. Maner (Three-Star General, Retired Chief-of-Staff for all U.S. forces in Asia); Edwin F. Black

(General, former agent for the Office for Strategic Services—OSS, Chief Administrative Aide to Allen Dulles, who was then the Director of the CIA), Walter McDonald (career employee of the CIA since 1975, and former Deputy Director over research in the agency). Robert "Red" Jantzen (former CIA Station Chief in Bangkok, Thailand); Earl "Buddy" Yates (began working with the CIA during the time of the beginning of U-2 spy plane missions over Russia, retired Chief of Strategic Planning for the U.S. forces in Asia, as well as the Pacific). It is alleged that the bank along with its extensive intelligence network were combining their resources to topple Australia's Labor Government. It is further alleged that the bank was laundering money for the CIA who were heavily involved in drug trafficking. In fact, the bank itself was thought to be a "CIA front". (Kessler, Ronald, Inside The CIA, pp 228-229) So, with all of these connections and special protections, why was Francis J. Nugan killed? The jury is still out, you might say, and we may never know. A former Senate Select Committee member involved in the intelligence investigation regarding the CI A's connection to the Nugan Hand Bank revealed: "They [the Nugan Hand Bank] perform certain services. If you want to move a little money around, or get some checks certified, you go to a bank to do it. Nugan Hand had a reputation for being very aggressive. They would take your money and wouldn't ask questions. What they [the CIA] were taking advantage of was a bank where employees were willing to extend the full range of services, no questions asked. It was for laundering and concealing money." (Kessler, Ronald, Inside The CIA, pp 229) So how did the Nugan Hand Bank get its start? Well, "in 1975 Michael Hand, a former Green Beret, coordinated the smuggling of a 500 lb heroine shipment from Southeast Asia's "Golden Triangle" to the U.S., by way of Australia. Soon thereafter, Hand began the Nugan Hand Bank. By 1979 the bank had 22 branches in 13 countries, and $1 billion in annual business. The Nugan Hand Bank has been linked by the Australia Narcotics Bureau to a drug-smuggling network which exported some $3 billion worth of heroine from Bangkok prior to June of 1976." (Ventura, Jesse, American Conspiracies, pp 115).

Keep this story in mind upon considering the power of the Federal Reserve Bank and those banks within its central system. In 1980 President Ronald Reagan appointed Alan Greenspan as Chairman of the Federal Reserve. Greenspan shortly thereafter affirmed the power of the Fed over that of our Government itself when he stated: "The Federal Reserve is an independent agency, and that means basically that there is no other agency of government which can overrule actions we take." (Ventura, Jesse, American Conspiracies, pp 169) Ironically, according to statistics provided by NORML, between 1970 and 2007, the increase in U.S. prison population skyrocketed by 547%, mainly due to drug-related offenses. The funds being made by the CIA created drug cartels which were being used not only to bolster the banking industry in the U.S. (roughly $250 billion per year in drug dollars funnel into our banks), but such trends trigger government expansion as well. (Ventura, Jesse, American Conspiracies, pp 114-115, 121).

Defense Secretary Robert Gates once referred to BCCI as "The Bank of Crooks and Criminals". At one point BCCI expanded into 78 countries, with over 400 branches, with assets exceeding $20 billion. One Senate report loosely reveals regarding BCCI's business relationships with government officials: "BCCI systematically relied on relationships with, and as necessary, payments to, prominent political figures." So, how did this behemoth get its start? BCCI was able to get its start with a little financial help from its friends, the CIA, and Bank of America, in Pakistan 1972. Norman Bailey, of the NSC (National Security Council) compiled a report regarding his findings while tracking terrorist group financing, wherein he stated: "We were aware that BCCI was involved in Drug-money transactions" (though the NSC had taken no action against them). A Time Magazine cover story headline in 1991 regarding BCCI stated, "World's Sleaziest Bank ". The same Defense Secretary Robert Gates, it was later discussed, failed to bring to light that he used BCCI as well. In fact, "Gates failed to disclose the CIA's own use of BCCI to channel payments for covert operations", according to British Customs Agent documentation. BCCI was the 7th largest bank on the planet at the time of its collapse, following the end of the Soviet-Afghan War. (Ventura, Jesse, American Conspiracies, pp 121.

This lack of transparency, and combination of government agencies in league with private banking institutions in order to covertly break the law are manifestations of how the Constitution is trampled daily by our government, and with the same net they are catching drug-related dollars and laundering them through banks; as well as netting the foot-soldiers who were responsible for making the money in drug sales on their behalf, ultimately. Ths creating an additional justification for forming new agencies of government (expansion + more loans from creditors = tax increases on citizens) whose mission is to target drug cartels, as well as expansion of prisons (25% of the world's prison population is in the U.S.). Michael Levine, an undercover agent for the DEA in the 1980's once expressed . . . "running a covert operation in collaboration with a drug cartel . . . is what I call treason." (Ventura, Jesse, American Conspiracies, pp 116).

Dennis Doyle, a former high ranking DEA agent stationed in the Middle East, stated the following at an anti-drug conference a few years ago: "In my 30-year history in the Drug Enforcement Administration and related agencies the major targets of my investigations almost invariably turned out to be working for the CIA." (Ventura, Jesse, American Conspiracies, pp 122) Where does it end? . . . When all of citizenry is either enslaved, imprisoned, or otherwise dead?

XI

THE GREAT RECESSION OF 2007

The Recession of 2007 was officially realized by the public in 2008 and recognized as such by the U.S. Government, finally. In 2008 the U.S. Government (i.e., The Federal Reserve) began the process of picking and choosing which global corporations were too big to fail! Lehman Brothers, one of America's oldest investments firms, did not make the "team". Whereas corporations such as AIG ($70 billion TARP award), Citigroup ($45 billion TARP award), Bank of America ($45 billion TARP award), JP Morgan Chase ($25 billion TARP award), made the top four on the "dream team". (Morris, Dick, Catastrophe, pp 76) [http://www.propublica.org/special/ show-me-the-tarp-money.]

  The top 20 financial institutions/corporations combined TARP award came to an astonishing $296 billion, as of March of 2009 (just the beginning, of course—Barrack Obama had been President of the

U.S. for just 3 months). With respect to the TARP, the New York Times reported a quote by John C. Hope III, Chairman of the board for Whitney National Bank in New Orleans, Louisiana, stated: "Make more loans? he asked rhetorically—as if the notion was out of the question.

He continued, "we're not going to change our business model or our credit policies to accommodate the needs of the public sector as they see it to have us make more loans." (Morris, Dick, Catastrophe, pp 77) In 2009, during the height of our current "Great Recession", in the U.S., the National Debt was a staggering $11 Trillion dollars (now the national debt is roughly $16+ Trillion dollars, 2013). Just to pay the interest alone, a monthly fee would top $26 billion (now $29 billion) which is laid at the feet of every tax-paying citizen. How does money our foreign power creditor(s) loan us break down within departments and agencies of government? In 2008 the rough estimates of the following agency annual budgets are as follows: Centers for Disease Control (CDC)—$6 billion; Coast Guard—$8.7 billion; Department of the Interior—$11.1 billion; Departments of Commerce—$8.1 billion; Education—$68 billion; Homeland Security—$42.3 billion; Housing and Urban Development—$52.3 billion; Energy—$23.2 billion; Department of Justice—$25 billion; Department of Labor—$49.6 billion; Department of Defense—$583 billion; Veteran's Affairs—$86.6 billion; Department of Transportation—$68.7 billion; The State Department—$18.9 billion. (Beck, Glenn, Glenn Beck's Common Sense, pp 31).

Two other U.S. Government Bureaucracy programs that have laden enormous burdens upon its citizens as well as future "heirs of debt" (their children and children's children), are a result of Medicare and Social Security. These two programs alone, created through Congressional

Legislation, in 2008 combined to a total liability exposure for future generations reaching $99.2 Trillion! (Beck, Glenn, Glenn Beck's Common Sense, pp 29) George Washington reminds us about the "frightful mein" that is 'government' in these words: "Government is not the reason, it is not eloquence, it is force; like fire, a troublesome servant and a fearful master. Never for a moment should it be left to irresponsible action." (Beck, Glenn, Glenn Beck's Common Sense, pp 43) In 2009 The Federal Reserve saw a way to seize the moment, even if it is one, they perpetuated, by calling in their debts. Whereas, through their member banks, they consolidated government bailout funding back at the Federal Reserve Bank and then charged interest on their loans (which are paid for through taxation). This is why the TARP bailouts did not free up national banks to make loans to the American populous and for a time it seemed as if no one was "worthy" is simply because money wasn't allocated sufficiently. Despite the fact that banks may "print money out of thin air" as Fed members, they were not given the "nod" to do so from papa Fed. In fact, $Trillions of Federal TARP dollars meant to bolster the national banking institutions (stolen from the American people, ultimately) were being held hostage at the Federal Reserve. Meanwhile, the media did all they could to downplay what was actually occurring.

    To show the world and the foreign power creditors he wants to "play ball", at a G-20 Summit in London, England, April 2, 2009, President Barrack Obama pledged his and the U.S.'s support for a "framework of internationally agreed high standards regulating financial institutions." President Obama stated this will result in "greater consistency and systematic cooperation between countries." President Obama further agreed to give over regulatory control of said institutions (SEC, Federal Reserve) to the FSB, Financial Stability Board and the IMF, International

Monetary Fund. (Morris, Dick, Catastrophe, pp 92) If foreign entities control monetary regulations officially for this country, then the creation of money, its valuation, supply, and demand will depend largely upon the FSB and its agents (the IMF) for America's economic and political survival. Those agreements are no less than a backdoor invasion, a contractual treaty of acquiesance and now all that is left is for the U.N. to be called upon by our government for policing "national emergencies" on our soil (constituting an actual invasion). What has happened to the confidence of Americans in financial institutions? It has been decimated by their manipulative tactics, and over-regulation of the institutions themselves, through government legislation enacted to bring our economy to a natural collapse. In as much as the lenders look the other way, so also will government as they go about with their varied agendas, combining to make that all-mighty dollar, all at the expense of us debtor citizens!

Let's consider the "Too Big to Fail" conspiratorial efforts demonstrating how government and the creditors work together to accomplish their goals today. In an unapologetic article written by Mr. Matt Taibbi called "Too Crooked To Fail", whose heading reads, respectively, "The Bank of America has defrauded everyone from investors and insurers to homeowners and the unemployed. So why does the government keep bailing it out?" I will begin with an exhaustive list why this question is so important, per the article: "Bank of America . . .

1. Participated in a plot to rig global interest rates.

2. Was fined $137 million for bilking needy schools and cities.

3. Used "robo-signing" evidence erroneously used to substantiate the loan application process.

4. Sold many worthless mortgages to unions, and State pension funds, bleeding the individuals who "buy-in" out of hundreds of millions in value.

5. Covered AMBAC and other insurance giants into insuring those mortgages, leading them into bankruptcy by fraud, as the insurers were spending hundreds on their faulty mortgage investments.

6. Controls over 12% of America's bank deposits (monopoly), which in fact, is contrary to Federal Law created to limit deposit size to a 10% control maximum.

7. Controls 17% of all home mortgages in the U.S.

8. Despite the $45 billion in government bailouts, such as TARP funds, its share price has fallen to below $10.00, a dramatic market value departure and was still falling through the floor for years following receipt of these loans.

9. In 2011, were allowed by the Federal Reserve to move very risky investments into the FDIC insured side of the company, thus putting the American people on the hook for a combined exposure reaching $55 Trillion!

10. Profited immensely thanks to the $26 billion in relief the Federal Government provided in an effort to assist homeowners who were duped, as it was tagged as a foreclosure settlement reserve. However, the bank was thereafter rewarded by our government with a legal waiver to escape several billion in pending lawsuits!

11. However financially toxic, is being over-rated by the Federal Reserve in order to perpetuate its "fiction of solvency".

12. Violated the McFadden-Pepper Act of 1927 and the Douglas

Amendment to the Bank Holding Company Act of 1956, which "make it illegal for a Bank Holding company to operate in more than one State." These violations continued unmolested by the U.S. Government until 1985; and then a Supreme Court ruling allowed for the bank's expansion into other States, officially." (pp 53-60).

The following statement by the author, Matt Taibbi, regarding this monster bank could not be more relevant, quote: "They lie, they cheat, and steal as reflexive as addicts, they laugh at people who are suffering and don't have money, they pay themselves huge salaries with money stolen from old people and taxpayers—and on top of it all, they completely suck at banking. And yet the State won't let them go out of business, no matter how much they deserve it, and it won't slap them in jail, no matter what crimes they commit. That makes them not bankers or capitalists, but a class of person that was never supposed to exist in America: royalty." (pp 60).

Does the government have programs that would put the U.S.'s own credit rating in the international community in jeopardy? Well, "in the years since the crash, the bank (Bank of America) has issued more than $44 billion in FDIC-insured debt through a little-known Federal Reserve Plan called the Temporary Liquidity Guarantee Program. The plan allows companies whose credit ratings are trashed to borrow against the government's good name—if the loans aren't paid back, the government (funded by American Taxpayers) is on the hook for all of it!" Bank of America "has also stayed afloat by constantly borrowing billions in low-interest emergency loans from the Fed— part of $7.7 Trillion in 'secret loans' that were not disclosed by the central bank until 2011." (pp 64) Elliot Spitzer, former Governor of New York recently commented that "for banks, the cost of capital is the key to success. So, by lowering their cost of capital to almost zero, the Fed has almost guaranteed that the banks will make big profits."

In the book, "The Indebted Society", co-authors James Medoff and Andrew Harless made the comparison of the U.S. Government's philosophy pre-1980's verses today's: "Thirty years ago, neither firms nor politicians used (or could use) massive indebtedness to justify their actions or inactions. Since 1980, firms, politicians and others have regularly used debt to rationalize conduct that has been damaging to workers and to the poor . . . Debt, directly or indirectly, has decayed the very soul of America." (Medoff, James, The Indebted Society, pp 265) Therefore, we see how government (agents of the creditor) and the lenders (local creditor institutions—banks) work in concert to expand their power, control, and wealth simultaneously to the detriment of the financial well-being of the citizens upon whose support they depend. It is the hustle of all hustles, crimes of all crimes upon which all others spring from! With respect to the growth of public and private debt held from the 1960's to 2000 investment strategist, Stephen Loeb, stated: "debt . . . is behind the pulsating growth of financial services . . . over the past fifty years, they have moved in lockstep as a percentage of GDP." The bubble of expansion shared by Insurers, Investment services and mortgage finance (working in league as one sector) grew by $17.4 billion between 2002 and 2004. This surplus in growth during those 2 years alone could have then satisfied our national debt and left a surplus of $1.4 Trillion, in theory. Do you think these organizations, public or private, have our best interests as a nation at heart? No, to them, it's just business.

In the 1990's the door to deregulation was left wide open. For example, "in 1996 the U.S. Supreme Court held in the Barnett Bank case that banks could sell insurance. In 1997 banks were allowed buy securities firms. In 1999, under the Financial Services Modernization Act (a statute resulting in the repeal of the Bank Holding Act of 1957) the Federal Reserve Board approved a merger between Citigroup (world's largest bank) and Traveler's Insurance Company." This policy of legislation created a new category of "Financial Holding Companies" (FHC). FHCs were allowed to own and control banks, security firms, and insurance companies under one umbrella, but "were also permitted to include non-financial enterprises." A year later, 500 FHC's had been created in the U.S. The door left open to such gross deregulation often resulted in "too big to fail mentalities" which created an environment for scandalization of the industry on a global scale. The Citigroup merger in question was the first trial FHC attempted, but its vast outreach extended into so many more organizations thereafter. In fact, "name any scandal of the last decade—Enron, Worldcom, Parlamat, biased [stock] research, and Citigroup's name will crop up."

As a result of the 1999 Financial Services Modernization Act, "Financial Holding Companies got a green light to own any kind of financial service company as well as investments in companies that had little or nothing to do with finance. They became catchall structures to mask risk investments in non-bank corporations. Another festering problem created by the Financial Services Modernization Act was so-called functional regulation.
The act claimed that each component of these new conglomerate institutions would be regulated by a different governmental regulatory body. This meant that different federal and state entities had oversight for

different components of the same business, yet nobody had full oversight for the entire institution's activities as a whole . . . So, functional regulation could more appropriately be called dysfunctional regulation." (Phillips, Kevin, American Theocracy, pp 293).

Does the U.S. Government "Bail Out" other countries in order to protect the ultra-rich few, at the expense of the majority of Americans? From 1982-1992, "the Federal Reserve and U.S. Treasury produced a relief package on behalf of the countries of Mexico, Argentina, and Brazil" due to an ongoing debt crisis to essentially avoid further injury to U.S. Banks. In 198 7, the Federal Reserve dedicated an immense liquidity in order to respond to the Stock Market dive, avoiding an impending collapse. This also quelled certain rumours about clandestine activities associated with a serious downturn in the market connected to the Fed itself. Between 1989-1992 the U.S. Government spends $250 billion to bail out hundreds of S & L's mismanaged into insolvency" (the Savings and Loan fiasco). During the years of 1994-1995 the "Treasury helps support (rescue) the Peso to backstop U.S. investors in high-yield Mexican debt."

In 1997 the "U.S. Government pushes IMF for rescue of embattled East Asian currencies to save American and other foreign currencies", as well as. "to save American and other foreign lenders." Then, the "Fed cuts U.S. interest rates to a 46-year low to reflate U.S. Financial and real-estate assets and protect the U.S. economy's newly dominant FIRE sector"—thus facilitating "post-stock- market crash rate cuts" (2001-2005). (Phillips, Kevin, American Theocracy, pp 289) Round and round, in and out of debt we go, and where it stops, we'll, history will tell us; but most will never know.

XII

THE GRASSY KNOLL

Taken from a TCP (Technological Capabilities Panel) report named "Meeting the Challenge from Surprise Attack", the following was presented to President Eisenhower on February 14, 1955: "We must find ways to increase the number of hard facts upon which our intelligence estimates are based, to provide better strategic warning, to minimize surprise in the kind of attack, and to reduce the danger of gross overestimation or gross underestimation of the threat. To this end, we recommend the adoption of a vigorous program for the extensive use, in many intelligence procedures, of the most advanced knowledge in science and technology." (Richelson, Jeffrey T., A Century of Spies, pp 295) In the spirit of the above report (which was a direct result of the attack on Pearl Harbor) let us consider the following memo which was ordered under President George W. Bush, Jr.

Wherefore, about one month after President George W. Bush, Jr. left office, in 2008, under Barrack Hussein Obama (then new President elect of the United States) a consequential memo was made known affecting the privacy and freedoms of every American. Its name is "Authority For Use of Military Force to Combat Terrorist Activity Within The United States."

Shortly following the terrorist attacks of 9/11, the Department of Justice secretly gave approval for the military to strike edifices where terrorists may be housed, such as "apartment buildings, and office complexes" inside the U.S. □s memo further granted powers for media suppression (Unconstitutional). Under this power of martial law "Military action might encompass making arrests, seizing documents, or other property, searching persons, or places, or keeping them under surveillance, intercepting electronic or wireless communications, setting up roadblocks, interviewing witnesses or searching for suspects." (Stormer, John A., Death of A Nation, pp 190).

Kate Martin, Director of the Center for National Security Studies think tank stated, regarding the memo in question: "In October 2001, they were trying to construct a legal regime that would basically have allowed the imposition of martial law." Also, Michael Ratner, a Constitutional scholar explained that the memo was nothing less than "Fuhrer's Law" and further stated: "The memo revealed how massive the takeover of our democracy was to be . . . [they] lay the groundwork for a massive military takeover of the United States in cahoots with the President. And if that's not a coup d'etat than nothing is." (Stormer, John A., Death of A Nation, pp 190).

John Robb, a management consultant, and former Delta Force Commander for the U.S. Military penned a manifesto called "Fast Company" which claims the ultimate results of the war on terror will actually be a "new, more resilient approach to national security, one built not around the State, but around private citizens and companies . . . Wealthy individuals and multinational corporations will be the first to bail out of our collective system (seek the remedy: Sovereignty), opting instead to hire private military companies . . . to protect their homes and facilities and establish a protective perimeter around daily life." Martin further eluded to the likelihood that the middle class would create their own "armed suburbs" to minimize the costs of security. (Rushkoff, David, Life Inc., pp 217).

The problem is, for those citizens who effectively pull out of the collective system, the U.S. Government has a habit of classifying them domestic terrorists. Thus, opening the door to Government intervention and invasion into private citizen's lives; also, it is easy for the media to sell the idea for oppression of citizens classified as "terrorists and enemies of the State" to the American populous after 9/11. On September 17, 1787, President George Washington penned a letter to Congress making this declaration regarding 'entering into society' (to become a debtor-citizen): "The friends of our country (creditors, security holders) have long seen and desired, that the power of making war, peace, and treaties, of levying money and regulating commerce, and the correspondent executive and judicial authorities should be fully and effectually vested in the general government of the Union: but the impropriety of delegating such extensive necessity of trust to one body of men is evident—Hence the necessity of a different organization.

It is obviously impracticable in the federal government of these States, to secure all rights of independent Sovereignty to each, and yet provide for the interest and safety of all—Individuals entering into society (giving up a measure of individual Sovereign-Creditor status, thus to become a debtor-citizen, and subject to the system of government in order to garner its 'protections'), it is at all times difficult to draw with precision the line between those rights which must be surrendered, and those which may be reserved ... In all our deliberations on this subject we kept steadily in our view, that which appears to us the greatest interest of every true American, the consolidation of our Union, in which is involved our prosperity, felicity, safety, perhaps our national existence ... the Constitution, which we now present, is the result of a spirit of amity, and peculiarity of our political situation rendered indispensable." (McGuire, Robert A., To Form A More Perfect Union, pp 225-226).

According to the author's (Robert McGuire) research regarding the founding of the Constitution of the United States, he concluded: "economic interests of our Founding.

Fathers did ensure, among other outcomes, that slavery would remain constitutionally legal until the Civil War and that holders of confederation securities (creditors) would benefit from the new government. But it is also true that there are many general aspects of the Constitution that do not appear to have been overtly influenced by partisan economic interests. Thus, from the perspective of not only Americans but also much of the world, our constitutional government is greatly admired and is not viewed as overly self-interested." (McGuire, Robert A., To Form A More Perfect Union, pp 212).

This is the best system we can hope for under the Constitution (despite the fact that we each are slaves to debt through taxation, for example). If only the Constitution was the real focus of government today. Wherefore, the constitutionality of law, policy, and legislation in government is the furthest "thing" from our democratically elected representatives' minds. Instead of "a spirit of amity", money, power and doing the will of their constituency, especially the creditors, is paramount.

Hence, the overwhelming necessity, demand, and predictability that the Lord of Hosts will return in all his glory, might and power, with the weight of his eternal sovereignty upon his brow, and the sign of his love for the righteous in the palms of his hands. Furthermore, New Jerusalem is the answer to the question over the separation of interests and citizenry in society, in order to establish the Kingdom of God upon the earth, under rule of the priesthood. Look for Zion, and be in the world, but not of it. It behooves us now to become agents unto ourselves, subject to God and the order of His house, alone; yea, for each of us to become the masters of our fate, and captains of our soul.

XIII

THE NEW MONEY

According to Douglas Rushkoff, author of Life Inc., the Corporation "was not a business or a government entity, but a combination of the two. Its government supporters—the monarchs had the authority to write the trade laws and grant monopolies; its business participants—the chartered companies—would enjoy the exclusive right to exploit them." The author continued . . ." the health of a corporation was understood purely in terms of money . . . Corporatism. Real things, such as human beings, land, and resources, only mattered in so much as they kept the credit side of the balance sheet bigger than the debit side. The underlying bias of corporatism would be that everything, and everyone, could be colonized (or made an asset to the corporation) for a profit." (Rushkoff, Douglas, Life Inc., pp 10).

Thomas L. Friedman, author of the book The Lexus and The Olive Tree, stated, "thanks to this democratization of finance, we have gone from a world in which a few bankers held the sovereign debts of a lot of countries, to a world today in which many individuals, through pension funds and mutual funds, hold the sovereign debts of many countries."

(Friedman, Thomas L., The Lexus and The Olive Tree, pp 53) How did we get here, how did a world of cultures, countries and differing opinions fall under one umbrella of influence and power?

Think of what is happening in this country and throughout the world, in fact and consider what Karl Marx and Freidrich Engels stated in the Communist Manifesto: "Constant revolutionizing of production, uninterrupted disturbance of all social conditions, everlasting uncertainty and agitation distinguish the bourgeois epoch from all earlier ones. All fixed, fast-frozen relations, with their train of ancient and venerable prejudices and opinions, are swept away, all new formed ones become antiquated before they can ossify. All that is solid melts into air, all that is holy is profaned, and man is at last compelled to face with sober senses, his real conditions of life, and his relations with his kind." The author explained that the significant contributors to the idea 'revolution' include "Engels, Marx, Lenin, and Mussolini, among others. The centrally planned, non-democratic alternatives they offered—communism, socialism, and fascism—helped to abort the first era of globalization as they were tested out on the world stage from 1917 to 1989. There is only one thing to say about these alternatives: They didn't work." (Friedman, Thomas L., The Lexus and The Olive Tree, pp 53, 84-85) Is Capitalism, what we have now to hope against, the answer?

Lee Hong Koo, South Korea's Prime Minister in the mid-1990's, made the following observation regarding our global capitalist system: "Now we say that 'market forces' dictated this, and you have to live with [those forces].

It took us time to realize what had happened. We didn't realize that the victory of the Cold War was a victory for market forces above politics.

The big decisions today are whether you have a democracy or not and whether you have an open economy or not. Those are the big choices. But once you've made those big choices, politics becomes just political engineering to implement the decisions in the narrow space allowed you within the system." (Friedman, Thomas L., The Lexus and The Olive Tree, pp 88-89).

With respect to the centralized system, Canada's Finance Minister issued the following declaration: "The sheer magnitude of Canada's foreign debt in relation to the size of the economy means that Canada has become excessively vulnerable to the volatile sentiments of global financial markets. We have suffered a tangible loss of economic sovereignty." (Friedman, Thomas L., The Lexus and The Olive Tree, pp 92) This is the common trend for countries throughout the world, now tied together under the banner of the World Court, the Central Banking System and United Nations and other Global Government consolidations. So, what is the new money? Oil and Drugs.

Ironically, so much "old money" is tied to and in control of it and has been for over a century. Though, markets affect price and are accountable to production, those who decide how much to produce and in what way the value of this commonplace commodity can be extrapolated and in the same vane manipulated, with the combined efforts of government(s), activist's groups, and corporations, as well as the media, but under the same banner is less a mystery as it is a travesty. If the war against terror is or isn't connected to oil, isn't the question today. It is rather, the excuse, the reason, the justification for policing the world's supply in order to gather this resource into the system's collection plate; as well as write legislation into law which subvert rights to privacy, property and every other so-called rights of citizenry under our Constitution, and Constitutions of other countries, and territories abroad.

    Professor Gordon Fellman made the bold assertion that "if the War on [Terror] is about terrorism and terrorism is the killing of innocent civilians, then the United States is also, a Terrorist." (Horowitz, David, The Professors—101 Most Dangerous Academics in America, pp 171) Sir Winston Churchill once warned "To build may have to be the slow and laborious task of years. To destroy can be the thoughtless act of a single day." (Rushkoff, David, Life Inc., pp 371) It would appear that the governments of the earth, and the creditors whose bidding they are adamantly resolved to, according to their interests—but in the name of the people—have been as chillingly thoughtless as man can be. What goes through the minds of men for such calamity to become commonplace and deemed necessary in civilized society?

    Perhaps it is we, the little people who have failed to understand, to comprehend that our lives matter far less in the eyes of the puppet masters. Whereas the agents of government are its strings, used by the puppeteer to pull us along to wherever, however, whenever our time comes. It is up to each of us to learn how to avoid the entanglements of society, the net of entrapments and pitfalls associated with failing to reach our potential as individuals. Following WWII, the OSS (predecessor to the CIA) coordinated plans with Sicilian Mafia and Corsican gangsters of Marseilles, France to play a "key role in the growth of Europe's post war heroine traffic . . . which provided most of the heroine smuggled into the United States over the next two decades." (Ventura, Jesse, American

Conspiracies, pp 114).

So many lives, so many families have been destroyed by the effects of those who pander and use illicit drugs. Our government declared a war on drugs in 1980 under President Ronald Reagan and then created the DEA— over 3 decades following the saturation of such insidious influences into society by the U.S. Government. In other words, our government needed 3 generations of users to build a sufficient network prior to justifying the expansion of government, through legislation and ratification of such into law, in the name of 'protection of the populous'. Consider these tactics perpetrated by our government as we try to learn why the U.S. Government has since the Civil War declared war on Slavery (and yet they have enslaved us all through legislation, passed during the war and because of the war); declared war on Facism (yet during WWII Congress and FDR passed more facist legislation fashioned into law than at any other time in U.S. history— many of the aspects of the New Deal specifically excluded Blacks, for example); declared war on Communism (yet during the Vietnam War so many rights of Americans were struck down once and for all, even our own President— JFK—who passed legislation that provided greater freedoms for every citizen, was assassinated, thus, the war on Communism was being fought against abroad—and for such ideals at home simultaneously); declared war on Terror (yet during Operation Iraqi Freedom, following 9/11, several more "ideas" were signed into law such as the Patriot Act which subvert the rights of privacy, property and many other individual freedoms—in the name of protecting America).

Now the U.S. Government, under President Barrack Obama, has declared war on guns, in order to protect American citizens from people who use them, sell them and lobby for their continued proliferation (despite the 2nd Amendment of the U.S. Constitution, our government is combining their power with the United Nations and other international coalitions in order to sell the idea to the world—thus exposing the U.S. citizens and citizens of other nations to invasions by foreign agents, doing the business of the creditors). Our military still occupies every country we ever dared to invade, in the name of these wars. What will be the next reason(s) to justify a new National Emergency be declared by way of Presidential Executive Powers, administering the continuance of Martial Rule upon the U.S. populous? And what won't the agents of the creditor do to assure the scene is set and game is afoot in order to put into motion some calamity affecting society in order to justify their own agency's existence and at the same time turn a profit for the creditors sufficient to grant further loans for our government (expansion)? The answer is . . . nothing. There is nothing they won't do!

Onward to Oil, to Energy . . . It was Henry Kissinger who once said, "control energy and you control the nations." Upon traveling in the U.S. in 1923, two prominent British visitors, E.H. Davenport, and E.R. Cooke, remarked: "Travel but a little in the country and you will gain the impression that the modernism of the United States flowed from its oil wells." (Phillips, Kevin, American Theocracy, pp 19) Though, "in 1919 only four oil companies had made the top sixteen ranked by assets: Standard Oil of New Jersey (Esso), Socony, Gulf, and Sinclair. By 1935 the number had doubled to eight: Esso (1), Socony (4), Standard Oil of Indiana (5), Social (10), Texaco (11), Gulf (12), Shell (15), and Sinclair (16), and the roll call for 1946 was quite similar." (Phillips, Kevin, American Theocracy, pp 37) Policing the world's energy supply began to be the aim of these companies in combination with government leaders and the military, here in the U.S.

as well as abroad, and it started to be so long before WWII.

In 1920 there was a rebellion in Iraq against Great Brittan's control over their natural resources, especially that of oil. Regarding this history, a professor at the U.S. Army War College revealed: "this was the first known use of air power as a constabulary . . . In time, the British expand the use of the RAF (Royal Air Force), sending it on all sorts of assignments. For example, it would bomb the tribes to soften them up for visits from the tax collector." (Phillips, Kevin, American Theocracy, pp 71) Per the author Kevin Phillips, in his book American Theocracy, "after WWII, when Washington gained precedence within the Western Alliance, the American CIA, not British Intelligence, stage-managed the 1953 overthrow of elected Iranian Prime Minister Mohammad Mossadegh. His principal transgression had been to nationalize the British-owned Anglo-Iranian Oil Company, although Washington also feared Soviet influence. Under the restored Shah, Reza Pahlevi, Iran then became a client state, principally of the United States. Anglo-Iranian Oil, although, readmitted at the head of a new consortium, was obliged to yield a 40% share to U.S. oil firms . . . by the 1960's the strategic importance of the entire Persian Gulf to the United States had been defined and upheld by a series of presidents beginning with Franklin D. Roosevelt." (Phillips, Kevin, American Theocracy, pp 73).

A late Scholar, Edward, made the following observation regarding a common theme among all of the great empires throughout history: "every single empire, in its official discourse, has said that it is not like all of the others, that its circumstances are special, that it has a mission to enlighten, civilize, bring order and democracy, and that it uses force only as a last resort. " (Phillips, Kevin, American Theocracy, pp 74) Consider this

Aforementioned quote carefully as we consider why we are at war in the Near East today, why we occupy Iraq (virgin territory for oil), Afghanistan (world's largest heroine crop), and soon to come Syria, perhaps. The Iraqi oil fields have been suspected by foreign powers for decades to be a relatively untapped mega-resource. A senior vice president of Italian Oil and Gas, Leonardo Maugeri once stated: "Only 2,300 wells have been drilled in Iraq, compared with about 1 million in Texas. A large part of the country— the western desert area—is still mainly unexplored. Iraq has never implemented advanced technologies—like 3-D seismic exploration techniques or deep and horizontal drilling—to find or tap new wells. Of more than 80 oil fields discovered in Iraq, only about 21 have been at least partially developed . . . It is realistic to assume that Iraq has far more oil reserves than documented so far— probably about 200 million barrels more." (Phillips, Kevin, American Theocracy, pp 77).

Iraq has long been viewed as a great opportunity for "Big Oil" to grow and expand production. An important oil analyst, Fadel Gheit observed: "think of Iraq as virgin territory . . . This is bigger than anything Exxon is involved in currently . . . It is the superstar of the future. That's why Iraq becomes the most sought-after real estate on the face of the earth . . . think of Iraq as a military base with a very large oil reserve underneath . . . You can't ask for better than that." (Phillips, Kevin, American Theocracy, pp 78) The United States, despite its much smaller population when compared with the collective nations of India, China, Russia, and continents of Africa and South America, consumes still 25% of the world's energy; meanwhile, our production of the fuel needed to support world consumption stands at 5%. By 2005 there were roughly 520 million

automobiles on the road and over 200 million are driven here in the U.S.

Our vehicle creation grows at a rate five times greater than the world's population itself. (Phillips, Kevin, American Theocracy, pp 37).

Lord Curzon of Great Brittan, after WWI, made the claim that an "A rab facade ruled and administered under British guidance and controlled by a native Mohommedan and, as far as possible, by an Arab staff . . . there should be no actual incorporation of the conquered territory in the dominions of the conqueror, but the absorption may be veiled by such constitutional fictions as a protectorate, a sphere of influence, a buffer state and so on." Perhaps, the same could be said for "post-2003 occupied Iraq." (Phillips, Kevin, American Theocracy, pp 79).

Following the Iraqi invasion of Kuwait in 1990, and in 1991 the subsequent mobilization of American military forces, President George Bush, Sr. declared as a rationale for war: "our jobs, our way of life, our own freedom, and the freedom of friendly countries around the world would all suffer if control of the world's great oil reserves fell into the hands of Saddam Hussein." (Phillips, Kevin, American Theocracy, pp 81) Also, Dick Cheney claimed that "once he [Saddam] acquired Kuwait and deployed an army as large as the one he possesses . . ." Saddam would then be . . . "in a position to be able to dictate the future of worldwide energy policy, and that gave him a strangle-hold on our economy." (Phillips, Kevin, American Theocracy, pp 81) What were some of the natural drives behind this line of thinking? In 1999, Dick Cheney, in a speech to the London Institute of Petroleum stated: "by some estimates, there will be an average of two percent of annual growth in global oil demand over the years ahead, along with conservatively a three percent natural decline in production from existing reserves." (Phillips, Kevin, American Theocracy, pp 89).

James Paul, of the Global Policy Forum provided the following oil production estimates for Iraq: "Iraq's oil is the world's cheapest to produce, at a cost of only about $1 per barrel. A gigantic 'rent' on Iraq's oil, during the decades of production, could yield company profits in the range of $4-$5 trillion . . . Assuming fifty years of production and 40% royalties, Iraq could yield annual profits of the top five companies, even in the banner year of 2003." (Phillips, Kevin, American Theocracy, pp 91).

So, why did we go to war in Iraq again? I'll let you decide. A Newsweek article described the "bad blood" that exists between European and American policymakers over the money oil should translate into, the currency it should be guarded by the Euro or the Dollar. The real battle was over "who gets to sell—and buy—Iraqi oil, and what form of currency will be used to denominate the value of the sales. That decision, in turn, will represent yet another skirmish in a growing global economic conflict." (Phillips, Kevin, American Theocracy, pp 93) Though, "in 1974 the U.S. Government convinced Saudi Arabia and OPEC to price oil in dollars, which to some extent put the U.S. dollar on an Oil Standard. Many so-called petro-dollars received in oil payments were invested through U.S. banks, recycling some of the benefits of higher oil prices." (Phillips, Kevin, American Theocracy, pp 290).

In 2001, Cheney and a league of strategists "poured over maps of Iraqi oil fields to estimate how much Iraqi oil might be dumped quickly on the market. Before the war, Iraq had been producing 3.5 million barrels a day . . . If Iraq could be convinced to ignore its OPEC quota and start producing at maximum capacity—the flood of new oil would effectively end OPEC's ability to control prices . . . Caught between falling revenues and

escalating debts, the Saudis, too, would be forced to open their oil field to

Western oil companies, as would other OPEC countries." (Phillips, Kevin, American Theocracy, pp 90) One Mr. Micheal Klare wrote that the U.S. Military "is being used more and more for the protection of overseas oil fields and the supply routes that connect them to the United States and its allies. Such endeavors, once largely confined to the Gulf area, are now being extended to unstable oil regions in other parts of the world. Slowly but surely, the U.S. Military is being converted into a global oil-protection service." (Phillips, Kevin, American Theocracy, pp 85-86).

Under the guise of "fighting terror" the U.S. also began to focus on the creation of permanent military bases in Senegal, Ghana, and Mali (West Africa). With respect to these plans the Wall Street Journal reported, "a key mission for U.S. forces [in Africa] would be to insure that Nigeria's oil fields, which in the future could account for as much as 25% of all U.S. oil imports, are secure." (Phillips, Kevin, American Theocracy, pp 85) David Frum, a White House speech writer, who authored President George W. Bush, Jr.'s political biography, in 2003 made the following statement regarding the connection between oil, terror, and war, whereas "the war on terror" was the mission of the U.S. Military in order to "bring new stability to the most vicious and violent quadrant of the Earth—and a new prosperity to us all, by securing the world's largest pool of oil." (Phillips, Kevin, American Theocracy, pp 83) Do you feel more secure? Is oil any cheaper for us here in the U.S., at least? Only you can prevent forest fires, don't leave it up to the government, they start em'.

XIV

THE CREDITORS

Andrew Mellon, Secretary of the U.S. Treasury (1921-1932), once stated with respect to debtors such as farmers and speculative investors, whose liquidation during the Great Depression, in his opinion, was necessary in order to "purge the rottenness out of the system". (Phillips, Kevin, American Theocracy, pp 276) Fast-forward a few years and weigh in on President Bill Clinton who, in 1993, upon considering the most pertinent factors that would contingently affect his re-election possibilities, while speaking with his advisor James Carville, asked in disgust: " you mean to tell me that the success of the program and my re-election depends on the Federal Reserve and a bunch of . . . bond traders?!" (Phillips, Kevin, American Theocracy, pp 283) Such was and is today the influence of the creditors foreign to this nation, through the legalization of a monetary monopoly here in this country—quite the contrary to the spirit of the U.S. Constitution—upon government and its "democratically elected officials". I think, however, it is important we take a moment to get to know just who these creditors are and why they collectively, perhaps, do what they do. Stephen Roach, Morgan Stanley's chief economist in 2004 stated regarding our National Debt, "we're not only outsourcing manufacturing to China and services to India, but we've managed to outsource our financing to Asia." (Ferguson, Niall, Cash Nexus, 347) From 2004-2005 East Asian nations made significantly large purchases of U.S.

Treasury debt (roughly $399 billion in 2004 and nearly as much in 2005) which resulted in a U.S. Financial Markets panic. Now in 2013 China alone owns $1 Trillion of America's national debt. A certain parallel is explained in the following story segment: "As the Korean comment ping-ponged around the world, all hell broke loose, with currency selling dollars for fear that the central banks of Japan and China, which held immense dollar reserves . . . might follow suit. That would be the United States worst economic nightmare." Not to mention "in 2005 Russia, Singapore, and Malaysia all announced small but significant shifts in the central-bank reserves from dollars to euros." (Phillips, Kevin, American Theocracy, pp 352)

We see how the central bank system in other countries can affect U.S. policy according to whether or not they invest in our debt (fiat money) or not, as well as directly impact our economy, our solvency and credit rating as a nation/corporation. Meanwhile, "the World Bank and IMF impose policy prescriptions on the nations to whom they lend money, all geared towards opening their markets to the interest of foreign corporations. When they fail to make their payments, these nations are subjected to structural adjustments that increase the resources they must commit toward repayment of the debt . . . The World Bank serves as the loan shark, while the IMF plays the menacing debt collector—backed by First World armies and their intelligence agencies." (Rushkoff, Douglas, Life Inc., pp 35, 37).

The essential models for creditor nations and international credit agencies were born in Europe, crafted after the Monarchy of the Royal Crown of England and Papacy of the Vatican. Let's take a look at the riches These entities have perpetuated as family firms, and heirs to the world's collective wealth. Did you know that among the 197 countries in the world, 51 of them fall under monarchy rule? Also, there are 35 different Monarchs in the world which consists of "26% of the world's states." (Cahill, Kevin, Who Owns The World, pp 25) there are six billion six hundred million people on the planet and only 15% of the world's population own anything at all, let alone land, which means 5 billion, 5 hundred million own nothing. (Cahill, Kevin, Who Owns The World, pp 3).

In the U.S., for example, 79% of the American population (308 million people in the U.S.) live in urban areas. (Cahill, Kevin, Who Own The World, pp 7, 89) Private home ownership in the U.S. (around 2005) stood at about 60%. (Cahill, Kevin, Who Owns The World, pp 10) The ownership of land is a significantly different matter altogether, in the U.S. and abroad. In Europe less than 1% of the population own 59% of all arable land. (Cahill, Kevin, Who Owns The World, pp 11) The primary landowner in the world by far (inasmuch as records permit) is the Royal Queen of England, Elizabeth II, holding nearly 6.7 billion acres, valued in average at $5,000 per acre, totaling roughly $33.5 Trillion in land value alone. That is one sixth of all land on the planet owned by a single monarch, head of state. (Cahill, Kevin, Who Owns The World, pp 14) For anyone who does not have "allodial title" (primarily held by governments and heads of state) ownership is reduced to mere tenancy. In the UK, for example, there are two types of land ownership made available. Freehold, which according to the UK's Land Registration Act of 2002, "is an interest in an estate in land, in fee simple" (Fee Simple means basically that freehold is an actual tenancy, the monarch or head-of-state being the true owner of the land). The Land Registration Act of 2002 explains further: "The Crown legal Estates under our management (Crown's legal advisor's) are in paramount ownership of the Sovereign, since "freehold" is itself a tenancy." (Cahill, Kevin, Who Owns The World, pp 18).

The Royal Crown's rule over the UK also extends to Canada, Australia, New Zealand, and many other states, providences, and colonies. (Cahill, Kevin, Who Owns The World, pp 18) In the U.S., ownership is a fiction; wherefore, all property, homes, and even the very lives (labor) of its citizens (subjects) are pledged as collateral to the money (debt) since we no longer operate on the "Gold Standard" or "shilling for shilling" basis. As far as legal records are made available, the other long-standing creditor, the Vatican, is considered the third largest land- owner in the world (however, much of their land owned in South America and elsewhere is not available to public privy). " The Pope, as head of the Vatican City State, is also a legal monarch. All land held by members of the Catholic religious order is ultimately held in the Pope's name. This comes to about 177 million acres." (Cahill, Kevin, Who Owns The World, pp 14, 33) These two states, The Royal Crown of England, and The Vatican rule, as monarchies . . . the entire world. The collective 35 monarchies own 25.5% of all land on the face of the planet.

In stark contrast to the prosperity of the few, particularly in America, for example, as it relates to wealth and land ownership, a report prepared by the "National Coalition For The Homeless" in 2007 revealed the following: "approximately 3.5 million people experienced homelessness in the preceding year. Single men comprised the largest segment of the homeless population (51%); while families with children (30%); single women (17%); and individual youths (2%) round out the equation." The rate of homelessness continues to grow in the U.S. and " according to the U.S. Census Bureau, in 2006, 36.5 million Americans were living in poverty" (roughly 12.3% of the U.S. population).

Remember that during the Great Depression, 25% of the U.S. population were unemployed (living at the poverty level or were homeless). Due to the Great Recession of 2007, which is alive and well now, in 2013, we are experiencing a national average of unemployment of around 8%, with pockets of unemployment reaching 16% in various regions of our country. We have come dangerously close to calling our Recession the Great Depression II, the sequel.

Are there other countries where the U.S. has participated in the operations and/or secret preparations leading up to a coup d' etat (in order to get control of natural resources, land)? The answer simply is, yes. Guatemala has struggled for independence on 3 separates occasions: from Spain in 1821; from Mexico in 1824; and finally, from the Federation of Central American States. Guatemala today is a country of "huge estates and landless peasants." Though, in the 1950's President Arbanz Guzman attempted to enact land-reform programs which were begun by the previous president. However, Guzman was "ousted by a CIA-inspired coup in 1954." It is estimated that less than .5% of Guatemala's population owns 90% of the country's farmland. (Cahill, Kevin, Who Owns The World, pp 265) is a common trend in most countries throughout the world, no wonder as to why. So, when we see our democratically elected leaders and the media stand before the world and declare the U.S. does not, and is not trying to police the planet, pause and ask yourself why are they lying about something so obvious? The answer is, because they are merely the mouthpiece, the "tool" for something much bigger than themselves, (and in their minds bigger than our Constitution) whom they have contractually signed on to protect and serve the creditor(s).

ABOUT THE AUTHOR

Eric Sanders, an MBA student at Walden University, specializing in Risk Management has been engaged in investigating claims, and looking at risk in the Global Insurance Field since 2000. Eric Sanders loves to seek the truth of our history, particularly American Presidents and U.S. Government. President Abraham Lincoln, a fellow Kentuckian, has always been one of his lifelong heroes. Born and raised on a cattle and crop farm in the hills of Liberty, Kentucky, work was something Eric learned to do in his large family, beginning at age 5 as master weed puller in the strawberry patch. Eric Sanders has an entrepreneurial spirit and is planning to open a business to support local tourism and area events. In addition to writing, his artful exploits extend to painting ocean scenes, learning other languages. Eric Sanders is also a talented singer and guitar player.

www.ingramcontent.com/pod-product-compliance
Lightning Source LLC
LaVergne TN
LVHW020438070526
838199LV00063B/4779